Praise

"As life is a journey so is this rich and thorough exploration of how we travel through that life. Starting with our earliest teachers, our family system, Dunion does a gorgeous job of weaving between the psychological and spiritual aspects of our development. He notes, at a time when we desperately need clarity and an understanding of the work at hand, that to become an adult is a developmental achievement, not a biological one. He offers us both a clear set of signposts so we can find ourselves on the map and a set of restorative practices to engage with to grow ourselves up both psychologically and spiritually."

Jennifer Cohen
Seven Stones Leadership Group
Executive Coach, Mobius Executive Leadership

"In his latest book, Paul Dunion suggests that the idea that you came from a perfect family is an illusion—and one that can be very difficult to swallow. He writes that being born into a family guarantees only two things: "You will be both gifted and wounded." He then commits his penetrating mind and wisdom to exploring the question of what it will take to keep "the good stuff from a family experience" and let go of the rest. Within every insightful discussion of a major family experience or trauma, Paul offers suggestions for healing, believing that each of us makes "a cosmic contribution to the greater good" when we take on the responsibility to learn and to heal. With *Family*, Paul makes a brilliant contribution to our living with greater understanding and freedom."

Jennifer Read Hawthorne, co-author of
Chicken Soup for the Woman's Soul and Life as a Prayer: Poems

"I enthusiastically endorse Paul Dunion's latest book on families, a remarkable contribution to psychotherapy and personal growth. As a family constellation facilitator, I have witnessed the transformative power of Paul's teachings and his profound understanding of human experience. Which his empathetic guidance, Paul delves into the complexities of family dynamics, offering practical tools to heal wounds and understand generational patterns. His approach, rooted in psychological principles and spiritual wisdom, fosters healthier and more fulfilling relationships. *Family* serves as a beacon of hope and guidance for navigating the intricate dynamics of family systems. Through his compassionate wisdom and his amazing storytelling, Paul invites readers on a transformative journey of self-discovery, healing, and growth. It is a testament to Paul's commitment to life, making it an invaluable resource for therapists, seekers, and those seeking harmony within their familial relationships."

Ester Martinez, PhD

FAMILY

In Search of Genuine Belonging

PAUL DUNION EdD

atmosphere press

Published by Atmosphere Press

Cover design by Josep Lledo

The conversations with clients are all true. Names and identifying characteristics have been changed or omitted to protect privacy.

Atmospherepress.com

Other Works by Paul Dunion

My Days with Emma: A Soulful Path to Elderhood (2022)

Wisdom: Apprenticing to the Unknown and Befriending Fate (2021)

Seekers: Finding Our Way Home (2016)

Path of the Novice Mystic: Maintaining a Beginners Heart and Mind (2014)

Dare to Grow Up: Learn to Become Who You are Meant to Be (2012)

Shadow Marriage: A Descent into Intimacy (2006)

Temptation in the House of the Lord (2004)

Dedicated to my extended family of origin,
especially my cousin Richard,
who became a loyal big brother,
and my paternal grandmother, Kitty Ryan,
whose soulful welcome held me in
a sweet embrace of belonging.

Table of Contents

Foreword

I'm not really certain about the actual nature of a family or what a family is. Since I come from a family and later created one, I know a little about the *How's* of family, the dynamics of family life. Whether you were abandoned shortly after birth in a hospital or brought home to a family celebrating your arrival, striving for emotional and physical attachment seems to be the order of the day. This longing for attachment would make you a lover, desiring to love and be loved, accompanied by genuine belonging.

We learn early about belonging through our needs for attachment and bonding. Whatever parents offer a child will be what the child identifies as the way of attaching. The child's ability to weave magic allows for abuse, neglect, and deprivation to all be seen as material for attachment. A child's psyche will not simply forgo a need for attachment.

Although there are different forms of attachment, the goal appears to be safety and security. The family is assigned the power to keep us safe or protect us from serious injury, pain and/or death. Once we bestow the life-preserving power to family, we automatically experience blind loyalty to our caregivers.

Our blind loyalty is extended to our caregivers regardless of the quality of care given. We can remain faithful to love, tenderness, deprivation, or brutality. On a deep, psychological level, any one of these energies is deemed capable of keeping us safe. Not making such a primitive decision would leave us facing an unmanageable peril, alone, vulnerable, and susceptible to whatever harm may come our way.

Of course, it is a set-up; the family will not be able to meet our needs for security, an enduring offering of genuine belonging, and love us exactly the way we wanted to be loved. There will inevitably be a dimension of longing for something more secure and more supportive of real belonging and love. It may be that security, belonging, and love are the major *How's* of a family.

Rather than perfectly meet our needs, family becomes a container for learning how we can become adults responsible for our security, belonging, and love. First, to acknowledge and address how the imperfection of getting what we needed hurt us. An old definition of the word *wounded* is "to bump into." For example, we either bump into too much attention or too little. I bumped into both. I became my mother's confidant and support before I was eleven. That's bumping into too much expectation and attention. Then there was motherly nurturing and affection which I bumped into too little.

Secondly, to let go of how imperfect your family met your needs. Remaining in protest of your familial imperfection leaves you taken hostage by the past. We let go when we are willing to take responsibility for apprenticing to the kind of security we want, the kind of belonging and the meaning of love we're willing to live.

An old meaning of the word *security* is "free from danger." It is fitting and appropriate to create an idyllic and allegedly danger-free environment for a child. Ironically, I have heard countless stories describing family as the main source of great danger. A child's psyche is not equipped to handle the inevitability of danger, or as Carl Jung suggested, "Life is a perilous journey."

Worth considering is how much our own attitudes, beliefs and choices place us in danger. The Sufi Kabir reminds us of the inner danger, "...when deep inside you there is a loaded gun, how can you have God?" It may be that the essential learning regarding security is learning to hold ourselves with an endearing compassion, especially when making mistakes.

Committing to make peace with life's 4 necessary conditions is what might support some measure of security. The 4 are: **non-permanence**, **suffering**, **death**, and **the desperate need to be loved**. These four expressions of being alive aren't going away and are asking us to consider making peace with them.

We think of belonging as a place or a group that welcomes us, exercises a curiosity about who we are and holds what they know with compassion. Initially, family often offers a sense of belonging. We know where we live and what we can expect from parents and siblings. The home is a place where we eat, sleep, work, and play. We hope home may be where we are received when hurt, lost, and discouraged. That kind of home will not happen perfectly, leaving us responsible for how we will carry defeat along the way, creating home for ourselves.

John O'Donohue reminds us of the work of belonging, "The most intimate belonging is Self-Belonging. True belonging comes from within. It strives for a harmony between the outer forms of belonging and the inner music of the soul." The imperfection of belonging will live with us, issuing a longing for a great welcome from external sources and inviting us to live with an interior welcome. I find myself more willing to ask, "Who in me continues to await my welcome?" Inevitably, I encounter some part of myself hungry to be gladly received.

Love is the third family dynamic and mystery. Our families will be a place where we either felt not loved enough or too loved. Not feeling loved enough will likely leave us feeling responsible for the absence of love, concluding that we are unlovable, while feeling too loved can have us feeling consumed and not free to express our uniqueness. Often times, our early decisions about how to love have a strong impact upon how we create a life. That happened between my mother and me.

By the time I reached middle school, I loved to see myself as an athlete; and in high school, I decided that a real athlete doesn't allow himself to get lost in books. Hence, I read only one book in high school, convinced that it was living testimony of my athletic prowess. My private war between sports and academia continued in college. Unfortunately, my poor study habits resulted in my flunking off the basketball team. To my chagrin, an armistice between the athlete and the student was forthcoming.

I soon fell in love with studying philosophy and six years later, I would be teaching philosophy. Fifty years later, my alleged abhorrence of schoolwork revealed a son's love for his mother. Following her completion of the eighth grade, my mother dropped out of school. She gave countless indications that she did not see the value of a formal education, including encouraging me to consider working at the local mill after high school.

It wasn't until shortly after my 70th birthday that I realized how threatened my mother felt about my education. I also realize how dedicated I was to easing her unrest about her limited education, so I loved her by creating a schism between my athletic endeavors and the classroom. I have come to appreciate how deeply a child can love a parent and begin creating life to prove it.

At 75, I continue to ask the questions, "Where do I come from?" and "What is that historical experience asking of me?" I continue to get to know the family I was born into and how I went about creating security, belonging, and love. My wish for you, the reader, is that you will make peace with how those three dynamics took place in your family of origin and how you are willing to remain an apprentice to them, shaping a life you believe truly matters.

Some security questions:

- How did my family of origin define security and what can I accept about that and what can I refine?
- How do I treat myself when I make a mistake, and it is similar or different from how my family treated me?

- Am I willing to make peace with suffering?
- Am I willing to make peace with dying?
- Do I exercise enough discernment when entertaining taking some risk?
- Am I comfortable letting go of what's out of my control?

Some belonging questions:

- How did my family of origin define belonging?
- How much of that definition do I take with me and how much do I let go of?
- Am I willing to belong to myself by living a self-examining life?
- Can I effectively discern whether I am known or not known by someone?
- Do I possess the courage to long for that place where I truly belong?
- Do I know how to belong without an excessive attachment for attention or acknowledgement?

Some love questions:

- How did my family of origin define love?
- How much of that understanding do I want to take with me and how much do I prefer to let go of?
- What do I fear when I open my heart and what is the fear asking for in order to hold an open heart?
- Am I able to be mindful of being loved and receive that love?

- Am I able to move beyond pleasing in my loving?
- What is love asking of me?

I highly recommend referring back to these questions as you make your way through the following pages. Or simply take a question or two with you as you read a particular chapter.

Chapter 1

Looking at the Family

"It is now clear to me that the family is a microcosm of the world. To understand the world, we can study the family: issues such as power, intimacy, autonomy, trust, and communication skills are vital parts underlying how we live in the world. To change the world is to change the family."

- *Virginia Satir* -

I thought I understood what a family was. There are parents and children, people go to work, and people go to school. There are rules, some spoken out loud and some you're simply supposed to know about. There are roles assigned without any clear stipulations of how they really operate. There are attitudes and feelings each member has regarding other members of the family. There are family legacies driving what people value and their choices from those values. Parents carry expectations that their children will live their own unlived lives for them. I've come to believe that the question of where I come from is one to address over and over for my entire life.

The current U.S. Census Bureau's definition of *a family* is "a group of two or more (one of whom is the householder) related by birth, marriage, or adoption residing together." It was likely easier to define a family this way prior to the Industrial Revolution when there was less mobility and family fracture as in a divorce. In his article "What is a Family?"

Professor Paul Amato points out that residency and biology are not relevant when defining a family. In fact, there are countless subjective ways to currently define *a family*. **For our purposes, the family will be defined as the family of origin, where two or more people decide to enter an agreement of mutual support, with one or more persons responsible for meeting the custodial and emotional needs of their offspring or adopted children.**

Birth – Announcing What's to Come

Our very beginning heralds the nature of the journey we call the human condition. The French Obstetrician Frederick Leboyer (1918–2017) reminded us that birth is essentially about loss. The infant is leaving the safest, most supportive, and most nurturing environment it will ever experience. If we're lucky, we get 9 months of gestation; and then we're hurled into an unknown world filled with a myriad of new stimuli and no longer automatically getting our needs met. A chord is severed, and we will never again know the unity of the womb.

I find myself asking, why would a soul embark upon such a perilous journey? Why take a trip that begins with loss and, because of its non-permanent nature, will constantly present us with loss? There certainly is enough ambiguity in the inquiry that we could simply surrender to the mystery of it. However, my curiosity gets the best of me, and I begin to ask what has been the most obvious task facing my 74 years on the planet? The task seems to be about learning and healing. Could it be that each of us makes a cosmic contribution to the greater good as we take on the responsibility to learn and to heal?

I've heard it said that the soul longs for participation in its boundlessness. My hunch is that the soul finds such an opportunity in the human condition, where learning about love, courage, freedom, compassion, and humility have no closure. There's always room for a bit more understanding and integration. This healing calls for mindfulness of some part of ourselves that we banish, determined to forget about, and the willingness to offer a welcome to what has been exiled. In such a welcome, learning is fed that which it needs in order to hold a larger vision of light.

I recently had such an encounter with a part of myself I condemned to the place where lepers dwell. Some time ago, I described my disgust to a mentor.

"Tell me more about what's going on. There's something obviously really bugging you," invited Ray.

"Well, I can hardly believe it. My friend Charles is chasing this English woman around the UK. She continues to swat away any overture he issues. She obviously wants nothing to do with him," I explained, with no need to hide my annoyance with my friend's choices.

"You obviously have some strong feelings about what your buddy is up to with this woman," Ray offered.

"Absolutely, I can't believe what a fool he's making of himself. He's so damn desperate!" I shouted, allowing my self-righteousness to fill the room.

"Desperate, you say. Hmm, do you know anything more human than desperation?" Ray asked, with the obvious declaration eclipsing the question.

I lost my breath, which didn't appear to be interested in returning until I intended it to do so. Its return only meant that I was gaining clarity about my need to issue disgust toward that which was extremely human. It was humbling, and I committed to interrupting the feeling of disgust when witnessing desperation, which I failed at as much as I succeeded in doing.

Then 20 years later desperation presented itself again, making the original experience with my friend clearer. A 70-year-old female acquaintance was engendering a romantic relationship with a 25-year-old male. My initial curiosity about why such a connection was happening was quickly suspended, assuming I was witnessing desperation. That was followed by deciding that it was about desperately wanting to be loved. Then came the wake-up call as the following rumbled through my head, "Do you have to make it so obvious?" Dripping from the question were piles of disgust.

My initial awareness that feeling desperate is what I had marginalized slipped easily into knowing that it was my desperate need to be loved that I banished. Just as I was willing to settle into offering a welcome to my desperate need to be loved, I felt a quake somewhere near my solar plexus as the heart of my disgust howled, "Your disgust is about the fear that your desperate need to be loved might be witnessed by others!" Fortunately, I knew that the fear of being witnessed by others was being generated by a lack of acceptance of my desperate need to be loved.

What about this desperate need to be loved? It's often presented in psychological terms as the early attachment need we all have. Could this desperate need to be loved, to unite with a caring other, be driven by the unity we once knew in our prenatal life? How likely is it that anyone, including the family of origin, is going to adequately meet this powerful need? It may be that we are the only ones that can come close to meeting this desperate need to be loved. Our healing might depend upon getting honest about this desperation and accepting the responsibility to take on the task, acknowledging how deserving we are of love. Of course, it will mean letting go of the myriad distractions that help anesthetize the longing to be loved. This will include all forms of hyperactivity driving us away from feeling our desperation as well as stopping the blame on our family.

There is no Perfect Family

Unfortunately, the idea that you came from a perfect family is an illusion and one that can be very difficult to swallow. What makes coming from a non-perfect family of origin so difficult to accept may be that it implies that somehow your family experience had less than a pristine impact on your character. Of course, there are no perfect people, and therefore, no perfect parents. I suggest that your parents did the best they could, and it wasn't enough. My best wisdom is that to be born into a family guarantees only two things; you will be wounded and gifted. Most people struggle to hold both offerings and become myopic, only considering the gifts or the injuries. Early primitive loyalty to the parent only drives a sustained vision of the gifts. While an obsessive need to focus on the injuries only leaves us victims of our family experience, seriously compromising personal power. Psychological wellness means being able to live in a family of origin story that includes both wounds and gifts.

The gifts may be an encouragement to develop certain talents and strengths, as well as following what is loved and cherished. It can be a gift to receive modeling from an authority figure regarding being responsible, honest, kind, and courageous. An ancient definition of the word *wound* is "banging into." We can either bang into too much or too little. Banging into too much can be viewed as emotional, physical, or sexual abuse. While banging into too little is what happens when there is physical or emotional neglect.

Julie, a 42-year-old primary school teacher, had been working with me for some time and was gaining more clarity about the gifts and the wounds she received in her family of origin. She was even able to identify a gift of the wound.

"It has been quite a journey starting with accessing the grief resulting from my mother dying when I was 12. My father struggled terribly with the loss of his wife and did whatever he could to distract himself from the loss, including neglecting my 2 younger brothers and me. He just could not show up for us. I began parenting my 2 younger brothers. That's not to say I knew what I was doing. I just made stuff up. You know, making sure there was enough food, making sure they got to school and didn't get into too much trouble," Julie recounted her early family experience with a measure of sadness and anger.

"I hear that you not only are honest about your experience; but in our last session, you suggested you were getting clearer about something positive that came out of the paternal neglect," I added, in the hope that Julie had enough emotional resiliency to address this issue.

"That's right. I do have more clarity about what you call a gift that came from the neglect. At 42, I have no problem being self-reliant. That's what the neglect gave me. It generated a large capacity for self-reliance. I see myself as very capable of identifying and meeting my own needs. Of course, the wounded element of the neglect is that I still struggle to ask for help and believe that someone might be a real resource for me," she explained, demonstrating a great deal of self-awareness.

"Didn't you mention that an aunt came into your life when you were around 15?" I asked, remembering that some relative had made a difference along the way.

"Yes, my Aunt Kate, my mother's sister, began to help out whenever she could. I guess she made a positive impression. She was a teacher, and I always wanted to be like her," she shared with her eyes moistening with gratitude.

"I remember you mentioning how much your aunt gave," I offered.

"I don't think we would have made it without her. She was kind, helped me pay the bills, confronted my father about his drinking, and taught me to drive a car," she expressed, her eyes lighting up with more appreciation.

Julie's psychological work had taken her to increased clarity about what was lost and what was given to her in her family of origin experience. She was accepting family life as a place to be wounded and gifted and asking for healing and learning about herself and about life. We began to address the issue of parentification, which, in Julie's experience, meant a loss of childhood as she attempted to parent younger siblings. We'll take a closer look at parentification in a future chapter.

We will be employing several lenses to view family life. They include **communication**, **problem-solving**, **decision-making**, **boundary setting**, **expressions of affection and nurturance**, **learning**, and **holding authority**.

Communication

How and to whom people communicate is a revealing window into a family. There are several dynamics, such as: Are children allowed to voice their opinions and wishes? Does the momentum of communication allow each family member to be heard? Is there a family member who tends to dominate communication? What material do parents inhibit when speaking to one another in the presence of the children? Are people engaged with eye contact when they communicate?

There are some basic skills that offer clear communication and are seldom employed in most families. The first is using the first-person singular pronoun "I" when speaking. It allows the listener to hear whom the speaker is talking about. It will also remind speakers who they are. It is a subtle way to support self-awareness. Most people speak in code with the usage of *everyone, no one, everybody, you, one,* and *some people.* The listening skill is simple acknowledgment. Examples include: "I hear you saying that you're not interested in attending Saturday's concert" or "It sounds like you are feeling sad about Pete's move out of the neighborhood."

There are 3 common patterns of communication that seriously interfere with effective communication:

Triangulation. This occurs when Albert has something to communicate to Bruce, avoids talking to Bruce, and brings the material to Carol. Let's assume these are three members of the same family. There are several reasons why Albert might bring his thoughts to Carol. First, Albert might not believe Bruce will hear him. Secondly, Albert might want feedback from Carol before speaking to Bruce. Thirdly, Albert might want Carol to communicate to Bruce for him. Triangulation has several unfavorable consequences. First, Albert might be soliciting Carol's sympathy and possible confirmation that Bruce's behavior was inappropriate. When this is the purpose of triangulation and it persists, the group will likely experience varying levels of divisiveness. Secondly, the rapport between Albert and Bruce is compromised as they do not have the opportunity to work out what might be challenging their relationship. Thirdly, the person in the role of Carol may take on the responsibility of listening to material that is not about them. Those family members often feel helpless and eventually resentful. Fourth, members in the role of Bruce can feel ganged-up upon, which can have an injurious impact upon their willingness to trust others.

Conflict. Conflicts or relational breakdowns occur under several different dynamics in a family. The first is that someone has an unmet need and does not know how to address it effectively. The second is that two people with different needs appear to be incompatible, leaving one or both people to believe that their needs will not be met. The third is that someone carries a story about a family member that results in dividedness and avoidance. The fourth is a values conflict where two people hold differing values, which leads them to believe that what they cherish will not be honored by the other. We will address these four kinds of breakdowns in a future chapter.

Family members resort to avoidance or attempts at influence when there are no clear guidelines for dealing with these inevitable dynamics in a family. Avoidance typically leads to resentment and compromised trust. Influence is driven by a need to be right and/or a need to win, eventually leading to weakened trust.

The No-Talk Rule. This rule is quite popular in most families. The rule operates as an implicit norm, suggesting that emotions, needs, and desires ought not to be expressed. The application of the no-talk rule becomes more rigid as stress increases in the system. The consequence is that family members cannot employ one another as viable sources of support.

There are typically 2 different consequences. The first is an Enmeshed Family where people simply buy into the illusion that talking about emotions, needs, and desires isn't happening because everyone is so happy basking in the harmony of the group.

The second is an Estranged Family, where members decide that what is important is their autonomy or individuality. These folks typically remain unconscious about the possibility that sharing emotions and needs can create deep emotional connections.

The first group plays family, and the second simply slips into what is important for each individual with no significant way to create a bridge to others. More will be said about these two ways of organizing family life.

Decision-Making

There are 4 ways that decisions can be made in a family. The first is *authority rule*, whereby the parents typically hold the authority to decide for the group. The benefit of authority rule is that it can be expedient and depend upon those holding the most responsibility for manifesting the decision. The tradeoff of authority rule is that it does not empower family members by enrolling them in the decision-making process. A consequence can be some form of sabotage by family members.

The second form of decision-making is *simple majority*. Hence, in a family of five, at least three members must be in favor of the decision. This process does represent more participants and can be expedient. However, those not represented again may resort to sabotage or at least resist implementation.

The third form of decision-making is *consensus*, whereby there must be a simple majority and the nays clearly stating they are willing to abide by the decision. If one nay is unwilling to accept the decision, then more discussion must take place. The benefit of this form of decision-making is that it enrolls the entire group, limiting resistance and sabotage. However, it can be time-consuming.

The last form of decision-making is *delegation*, whereby either the designated authority or the entire group defers to one or two members to make the decision. The assumption is that those delegated possess some interest and/or competency, which entitles them to decide for the group. The key is for authority figures to be clear about what decision-making process they will employ and possibly explain why. When this clarity is offered, typically regardless of the choice of decision-making, resistance and sabotage diminish.

Boundary Setting

We can look at the constellation of a family based on the employment of boundaries in the system. Boundaries tell a family's story about how safety is provided, how much emotional closeness is tolerated, and how much individual expression will be permitted. Some families utilize very permeable boundaries, which do not effectively separate family members from one another. Each person is encouraged to share the same beliefs, feelings, and values as everyone else. Individual differences are ignored and frowned upon, and conflict is also heavily avoided since it would represent individual preferences. We'll look more closely at permeable boundaries as we explore the Enmeshed Family.

Some families employ strong or non-permeable boundaries, such as an Estranged Family. These boundaries tend to significantly separate family members. This family views emotional distancing as advantageous and supportive of individual autonomy. Families will lean toward exercising permeable or non-permeable boundaries. There is no way to employ boundaries perfectly. Boundaries are either supporting the group a bit too much or supporting individuals too much. At best, we can evaluate the status of our boundaries and remain corrective.

A family can employ light-permeable boundaries, moderate ones, or extreme permeability. The same is true for non-permeable boundaries. They can be lightly non-permeable, moderately non-permeable, or strongly non-permeable. It is not helpful to employ a pathological lens when viewing the status of boundaries, and considerably misleading to suggest that we can get our boundaries just right.

However, a third category of boundary that can be practiced are semi-permeable boundaries. The permeability or the pervious nature of a boundary is generated by discernment. It takes practice to decide, in any situation, just how much of what is coming at you to allow in. With enough discretion, you can decide to accept a little of what you're hearing, a larger amount or none.

Holding Authority

Parents who take the holding of authority in the family seriously are usually acquainted with what to avoid when exercising authority. They at least know they do not want to abuse their authority, and they also may not want to abdicate it by holding little or no authority. In the inevitable expression of imperfect parenting, both abuse and abdication will take place and quite often move in one direction to compensate for the other. Even when there is no physical or sexual abuse of children, there will be bouts of emotional abuse. The latter can happen through blaming, shaming, yelling, demanding, bullying, and various forms of dominating and withholding.

It can be helpful to identify what to do when holding authority as opposed to simply knowing what to avoid. I like the think of holding authority as an act of authoring a family and helping members to also participate in authoring the family. There are at least three dynamics comprising authoring a family.

The first is *boundary setting*. Establishing effective boundaries sets limits regarding support for safety, health, and group cohesion. They can range from schedules for sleep, screen time, mealtime, task time, and social time to expectations regarding household chores and unacceptable behavior and resulting consequences. Before setting a boundary, I highly recommend asking if the child's behavior places him or her, others, or the environment in some danger. If the answer is no, then it might be best to suspend a boundary in favor of the child's self-exploration.

The second authority dynamic is *problem ownership* which can have a dramatic impact on what it means to hold authority. Problem ownership defines a problem between two people as someone having an unmet need, and the person with the problem is the person with the unmet need. It becomes only too clear, too quickly, that most problems arising in a family belong to parents and not children. Children typically do not have unmet needs pertaining to taking a shower, making their beds, cleaning their rooms, feeding the dog, etc. Problem ownership asks parents to call off criticizing, lecturing, and threatening and to get honest about speaking to their unmet need, which may be accompanied by a request.

The third dynamic is *modeling living in integrity*, which means being committed to making choices that reflect your values. It means that parents need to get acquainted with their values and be honest about actions that are not compatible with their values. This might mean making amends (an apology with a commitment not to reproduce the behavior) to their children when the parent treats the child in a manner that has the parent stepping out of integrity.

Expressions of Affection and Nurturance

Families vary greatly regarding expressions of affection and nurturance. Typically, parents reproduce for their families what they experience in their own families of origin. Where there is hugging, kissing, holding, cuddling, and gentle touching, effective boundaries are needed. The boundaries are created based on meeting the needs of the children and not the parents. That is, some children may be very open to a good deal of affection, while others are fine with very little.

Boundaries are too weak or permeable when parents are either engaged in overt expressions of sexuality or covert gestures or glances. Fathers need permission to feel attracted to their maturing daughters while employing effective boundaries. Only too often, fathers either violate the child's sexual boundaries or issue strong non-permeable boundaries, disallowing any form of physical contact. The latter response is often motivated by the father feeling shame for his attraction. Teenage daughters often explore their relationship with the opposite gender by flirting with their fathers. Solid fathering can result as a father is receptive to the flirtatious overtures and maintains effective boundaries supporting tenderness, warmth, and being complimentary of the daughter's beauty.

Learning

Learning is an ongoing dynamic in a family, which can be supported or hindered. Parents do not support the learning of children by preaching and lecturing, although those means of inducing learning are quite common. There are several ways that parents can best encourage learning for their children. The first is modeling. When parents demonstrate their own curiosity and confusion, children have a map illustrating what it means to be honest about not knowing and initiating a thoughtful inquiry. It is also very helpful to encourage a child's curiosity and not feel the need to supply answers to all their wonderings.

Dominic, a 42-year-old social worker, was describing the mismanaging of learning that went on in the alcoholic family he came from.

"There was a tendency in my family to describe the *what* of a task with no instruction as to the *how*. So, when I turned 7, my father told me that I could help him wash the car. He handed me the water hose and said I should begin, and he would join me shortly. I decided that it was probably best to start with the inside of the car before spraying down the outside. I opened all four doors and proudly watered down every inch of the car's interior. Well, you can imagine the reaction of my alcoholic father upon seeing my car-washing approach," Dominic recounted, the both of us laughing hysterically at what can happen when the *how* of a task is not clear.

Storytelling is also a helpful tool in support of learning. Stories that describe a parent's fumbling and seeking help are especially useful. Parents can also allow their children to learn from the concrete and logical consequences of their choices. Concrete consequences include any result happening because of an interaction with the natural world. Examples are getting wet because of not wearing a coat, falling when running on ice, getting stung when poking a beehive, going to bed late and feeling tired the next day, and refusing to eat dinner and feeling hungry. Parents tend to mitigate the opportunity to learn from concrete consequences in fear that a child might get seriously hurt. Hence, it is important to exercise discernment when deciding to allow a child to learn from concrete consequences.

Logical consequences are the emotional and behavioral effects a child's action can have on others. A child excludes a friend from playing and experiences a retaliatory response from that friend. A child gets into bullying and finds that he is being avoided by his peers. A child badmouths his mother and finds himself in a time-out.

Family Roles

We can look at the roles children take on in a family. These roles appear to have an archetypal nature; that is, their energy seems to address something essential to the human condition. The roles are often described as **Hero** (*White Knight*), **Lost Child** (*Magician*), **Scapegoat** (*Black Knight*), and **Mascot** (*Court Jester*). As we shall see, each of these roles attempts to make an offering of love to the family. The Hero offers achievement and success; the Lost Child offers peace and quiet; the Scapegoat offers a negative distraction from the pain carried by the parents; and the Mascot offers a playful distraction. We will explore each of these roles more closely in future chapters. For now, let's note that each of these roles has value, and what ultimately hurts children is being locked in rigidly to one role. Wellness is a measure of how much flexibility a child has to move from one role to another. As stress increases in the system, so does the child's rigidity attach to one role.

Betrayal – A Way Home

What does it take to keep the good stuff from a family experience and let go of the rest? Letting go is not quite like cleaning the basement accompanied by a trip to the town dump. Soulful letting go happens as we carry toxic legacies and familial injuries with more mindfulness and compassion, which depend upon the courage to betray an early allegiance. This primal loyalty has us viewing parents through a pristine lens, dispossessed of all blemishes.

A child's psychological stability is reinforced by seeing parents as powerful, intelligent, and righteous, fully capable of offering the best care possible. However, such a sanitized account offers a very distorted view of reality. It takes courage and an abiding commitment to not only get honest about our parents, but also refuse to hold ourselves responsible for how they treated us. The way to this more realistic version of the past is by betrayal, betraying the blind loyalty we held as children. It may also feel like betraying our parents, especially if there is any hint of viewing our parents as unblemished.

Taking a mythic view of the Judeo-Christian origin myth can offer valued insight regarding the role of betrayal in a family. Adam and Eve are told by God, their father, not to eat the fruit of the tree of knowledge. Are we being told that fathers may be reluctant to accept that their children might know as much or even more than they do? Eve decides to eat the fruit. We might say that she is betraying her blind loyalty, the belief that the father only has her best interest in mind. She pays the price of being kicked out of the house. From a mythic perspective, she must now create her own beliefs and values; that is, she can become an adult. If she remained in the

Garden, then she would continue to be an obedient child. Is the myth suggesting that growing up is risky business? Might it also be putting forward the consideration that adulthood is likely only achieved by a measure of betrayal?

A Blessing for Family

The ancients suggested that families are those with
whom we are familiar. That likely is our soul task,
to become more familiar with those who reared you.
However, such familiarity will call for the termination
of an early loyalty – a blind loyalty.
This original faithfulness to your caregivers rendered
them almost godly.

Infused with the magic of childhood, this boundless
allegiance promised safety, love, and comfort.
When the guardians stumbled, leaving you
feeling hurt and alone, there was only one explanation
you could live with – there must be something
fundamentally wrong with you.
There was no other path to security.

There would be a myriad of voices desperately
trying to make sense of the pain and neglect.
Voices continuing to uphold the alleged
steadfastness of character, describing your parents.
"I was stupid clumsy, selfish, inconsiderate,
and mischievous."
Each declaration aimed at explaining how you feel
so aggrieved while having wonderful parents.

You cannot hold your essential goodness unless
devotion finds a new home.
You had imperfect parents who created an imperfect family.

You can now restore their humanity and your
unconditional deservedness.
They may not know the restoration of their humanity as a gift.
They may feel betrayed as you humanize them.

Devotion must now find a new home,
one that dwells in your heart.
One that heralds the news of your inherent goodness.
Be familiar with where you come from and
then familiar with who you are, your injuries, your fumblings
and your gifts – all in honor of your humanity.

Chapter 2

The Enmeshed Family or Too Much Family

"Away from them, I realized that they formed a united circle, or rather, a net, in which they were enmeshed together. I was the only one out of it. Being near them made me feel more alone."

- Oscar Lewis -

An Enmeshed Family diminishes the value of individual members while prioritizing the well-being of the group. The enmeshed imperative is: Are you giving enough to others? Weak boundaries masquerade as expressions of closeness and togetherness. There is a way to be, and individual family members are encouraged to figure that out and make It happen, in honor of the group. Before taking a closer look at the prevailing characteristics of an enmeshed family and recommended strategies for healing, it may be helpful to stress the importance of understanding the imperfect nature of families.

Parents of an Enmeshed Family likely recreate the family configuration they were raised in and know. We can say that what they understand is that family is constructed with permeable boundaries. Boundaries that do not effectively separate and honor the unique aspirations, needs, and beliefs of its individual members. It is somewhat of a natural phenomenon for parents to not only create what's familiar but to err on the side of too much support for the group or too much for each separate member.

More sophisticated boundaries are semi-permeable ones. which are established with discernment assessing whether the autonomy of individuals needs more support or the cohesive connection to the group. The process needs to remain corrective. A group doesn't do support of the whole and support for individuals perfectly. It calls for commitment, perseverance, and enough humility to fumble with the evolving nature of a family.

Characteristics of an Enmeshed Family

Weak boundaries. Boundaries in an Enmeshed Family can be extremely permeable. Permeability inhibits how family members distinguish themselves from others in the family. Members get effective at reading what others in the family expect. It becomes only too easy for family members to feel entitled to influence and control others. Hence, enmeshed families typically experience a higher incidence of both emotional and sexual incest.

I was working with Joan, mother of three children and a devoted kindergarten teacher. When introduced to what it means to come from an Enmeshed Family, she came to the edge of her seat, "Oh my God, I thought we were just really close!"

"The members of your family may have felt close to each other, and it does sound like the boundaries in the family were considerably permeable," I suggested, wanting to support Joan's introduction to enmeshment.

"Well, the more I think about it, the closeness mostly happened before adolescence and young adulthood. I've recently noticed that several of my siblings get rather critical with a number of my choices, workshops I go to, and people I choose for friends," she offered, her voice trailing off with her gaze moving down and away.

"Joan, I wonder if you're having some feelings about your relationship with your siblings," I suggested, hoping she might feel invited and comfortable enough to give a voice to her feelings.

"It's just something my younger sister Sally told me recently about our older brother. It's hard to believe it happened, and I know that Sally would not make such a thing up," pausing, with her jaw-dropping and lips quivering, "Sally said that our brother Ted sexually abused her when she was 13," Joan divulged.

"How do you feel about telling me?" I asked, wondering if she might feel like she betrayed Sally.

"I feel nervous and I'm glad it's coming out. I don't remember Ted ever touching me inappropriately, but I often got the feeling that he was peering as I left the bathroom after showering. Do you think what happened to Sally has anything to do with the enmeshment of the family?" she wondered, eyes widening, and her tone genuinely curious.

"Well, it's likely. In an Enmeshed Family, no one truly owns their own body or for that matter, their own mind," I pointed out, seeing Joan lean forward with interest.

"I'm not sure I understand what it means not to own your own body," Joan offered.

"When boundaries are too thin or permeable, the message is that what you call yours is also ours, ours to access and claim in some way. What belongs to one member belongs to everyone. That could be your mind or your body," I explained, noticing Joan gently nodding as if what she was hearing she already knew.

Our work focused on Joan learning about semi-permeable boundaries and committing to employing boundaries in her own family that supported individual differences while building a trusting and cohesive unit.

Externally referenced. Family members are encouraged to read the needs and dispositions of others in lieu of their own. Love is understood as attending to others and the attention is typically driven by hypervigilance. This exaggerated focus on others happens because it's a violation of family norms if someone focuses on themselves, hence everyone depends upon others to pick up on non-verbal cues regarding needs and upsets. Family members easily succumb to feeling guilty if someone's discontent was missed. Often, folks feel low-grade anxiety about the possibility that someone other than themselves was not properly supported.

Diminished support for autonomy and individuation. Being self-focused is frowned upon. Getting clear about one's own values, needs and desires can be seriously compromised. One consequence is that personal identity can be undermined, leaving family members feeling separated from themselves. They know more about who they are as related to other family members rather than feeling solid with their interiority. Their identity is strongly planted in family roles.

The psychological merger that characterizes an Enmeshed Family often has a here-and-now experience being haunted by some historical family dynamic. George came from an Enmeshed Family where he found himself traumatized in a family triangle. He discovered that when he was in a current triangle with no unfavorable consequences for him, he felt the heartbreak of the original triangle.

"My two sisters were kind of raised by my mother, while I and my younger brother were raised by my father when he was available," George's voice trailed off as he mentioned his father.

"I'm wondering if you saw your sisters getting more parenting from your mother than you received from your father," I offered, wondering if he might be carrying feelings of loss.

"Yes, my father wasn't around much, but the big deal was I

had no idea how to break into the triangle with my mother and my sister Louise. I mean, they were tight, and I just could not get connected to my mom, but I don't want to take anything away from them. They had a good mother-daughter thing, you know what I mean?" George added, seeming to mitigate his loss in favor of what his mother created with his sister.

"I hear you don't want to diminish the relationship between your mother and your sister. And it's okay to feel the loss of your mom," I encouraged.

"Yeah, I hear you. I'm reminded of what you mentioned about these triangles getting reproduced. You know, the one at work with my boss Peggy and my colleague Maureen. Sure feels the same," he admitted with a note of anger, leaving me feeling a bit confused.

"I get that you've been in a triangle with two women again. But, my understanding is that the outcome of this triangle at work was quite different than the one in your childhood," I suggested, given the information I had.

"Well, both triangles felt awful. I can't tell you how many times I witnessed Peggy and Maureen doing their female thing together. They have been really bonded," stressed George.

"George, I've got to tell you that I have a different take. Didn't Peggy let go of Maureen and promote you?" I asked, seeking confirmation of his experience.

"Yes, yes she did. I don't know, nothing about the whole thing felt right," he added, casting his gaze downward.

"Okay, so what I recall is that Peggy has been very clear about believing in you and supporting you. Sounds like the kind of boss we all might want to have," I proposed, curious about how much of the energy attached to the original triangle he might have dragged into the current one.

George was willing to interrupt his protection of his mother and his sister and access his anger and hurt about feeling marginalized in the family. As he was able to access the loss and grief related to his mother, he began to appreciate how much Peggy remained a professional ally.

Love means being self-sacrificing. Efforts to support oneself can be viewed as unloving. Consistent self-sacrifice typically yields accusations that others are not doing enough with an attachment to the illusion that others can make you happy. Being self-sacrificial also tends to lead to resentment as a family member awaits a payoff for sacrifices rendered.

Conflict avoidant. Family members are encouraged to remain conflict-avoidant since a conflict may have an unfavorable impact upon others. Consequently, family members do not learn how to reach conflict resolution. The typical approach to conflict is avoidance. However, avoidance tends to lead to case-building and narrative confirmation. Case-building happens as avoided emotional material builds and we build a case against a person's character. Narrative confirmation occurs when we might decide that someone is insensitive, and we tune into any behavior that might support our narrative about their insensitivity.

Learn to become caretakers. Family members learn that they are responsible for the well-being of others and are willing to remain self-neglectful to meet the family imperative of caring for others.

A tendency for the children to be parentified. Parentification of children happens as they are encouraged to either parent themselves, parent siblings, or reverse roles and parent one of the parents. Because of the weak boundaries coupled with the heartening to become caretakers, parentified children in an Enmeshed Family often experience an early role reversal, parenting one of their parents.

Fear of abandonment. Because members have a compromised relationship with themselves, their greatest fear is to be rejected or abandoned by others. This fear often carries an acute sensitivity where there is little resiliency for tolerating the unfavorable responses of others. To mitigate others being upset with them they exercise a strong need to please and be liked. As Emily learned about her fragility when it came to others being angry at her, she understood how she coped.

"I made up the story that I was a very likable person. In fact, I always said that people just naturally like me," Emily explained with a sheepish smile.

"I'm interested in your smile. What does it say?" I asked, in the hope that she might pause and consider the smile's message.

"Well, if I'm really honest, the truth is that I give a lot, I mean a real lot in the hope that my giving will be able to fend off unwanted anger, disappointment and frustration people might have with me. You know, I'm starting to think that it's not about how much I give, I think that people might just feel too guilty, to be honest with such a kind person. They might not tell me that they are angry at me, but they also aren't building anything truly intimate with me," Emily shared, revealing how much she was willing to get honest with herself.

Emily soon learned how much she neglected herself and how much energy she put into taking people hostage with her exorbitant levels of giving. She also became clearer about the possibility of becoming one of the recipients of her giving.

Encouraged to feel guilt, shame, and anxiety. These feelings are encouraged as a member might stray from the family mandate to remain focused on supporting the comfort and happiness of others.

Compromised personal agency. Once family members have internalized the family imperative to serve the collective and not themselves, they are prone to becoming excessively passive when it comes to knowing their desire and acting toward its satisfaction. They are more comfortable waiting for others to care for them.

Deluded about genuine emotional intimacy. Members of Enmeshed Families are usually convinced that enmeshment is synonymous with emotional intimacy. If we define emotional intimacy as the unity of two separate and unique individuals, it becomes clear that enmeshment is masquerading for authentic unity. When the denial of the self is seen as loving, it can be extremely difficult to learn what it means to choose oneself, an essential building block of real intimacy.

Guidance for Healing

It is critical that folks who come from an Enmeshed Family understand that there are no perfect families. Enmeshment was simply the system's way of attempting to coalesce and cope with the tension of generating unity with unique individuals. It is helpful to introduce the notion that the only option is to come from an imperfect family. It doesn't mean that someone having been reared in such imperfection is damaged goods. It only means that life is a great deal about understanding where you come from, as well as what healing and learning your past is asking for.

Let's look at some of the restorative interventions an enmeshed beginning might ask for:

Permission to grieve. As you explore the losses that naturally accompany being raised in an imperfect and Enmeshed Family, it is healing to access the sadness and anger associated with these losses. Losses may be as practical as no door to your bedroom or no lock on the bathroom door, depriving privacy. You may have felt shame because you were called to an ideological path not compatible with that of the family.

Betrayal of the family mandate. Simply exploring how your Enmeshed Family did not reach some idyllic status can feel like a violation of loyalty. The key is to not view your parents as bad because they were instrumental in creating an imperfect family. They too came from an imperfect family. Betrayal might simply mean that you are entitled to grow out of an attachment to dysfunctional patterns, an entitlement that can serve your children and their children.

Permission to be internally referenced. This simply means that a healthy relationship can begin because we are acquainted with the person we bring to the relationship. We can know our preferences, our beliefs, and feelings. Our interior world is what we can know and have some measure of control over. We can be internally referenced while being empathic, understanding, and negotiable.

Boundary education. Members of Enmeshed Families live with excessively permeable boundaries. It is important to broaden your understanding of both non-permeable and semi-permeable boundaries. The former is needed when there is an actual imminent threat to safety. However, it is semi-permeable boundaries that support a higher level of relational functioning. These boundaries have a dual purpose. They support our safety or uniqueness while allowing us to be accessible to others.

Redefining love and intimacy. Members of Enmeshed Families need help to let go of understanding love and emotional intimacy as characterized by persistent self-sacrifice and caretaking of others. An important lesson is learning to redefine love, such that both giving and receiving get top billing. They need to add the act of receiving to their understanding of love, as well as making requests of others, and be introduced to their responsibility to support self-love. They also need to understand that when self-love is compromised, they run the risk of passively waiting for others to love them in lieu of loving themselves. Gaining clarity about necessary vs. unnecessary self-sacrifice becomes an essential relational competency. Giving new meaning to love calls for therapeutic support and guidance, and the willingness to stumble with such an immense and honorable undertaking.

Managing conflict. Because avoidance was the pattern for dealing with conflict, they will need to learn to interrupt catastrophizing the presence of conflict. They can acquire conflict resolution skills and come to accept conflict as a natural phenomenon in healthy relationships.

Permission to live from desire. They will need to be encouraged to be curious about their desire, feel it, and pursue it as an essential way to engage in life. They will need to be reminded that living from their desire is not unloving. It is simply the most natural way to welcome oneself into life. It can be helpful to remember that as you live your desire, you can be curious about the desire of others.

It is important to accept enmeshment as one way to cope with the tension of remaining connected to the group while connected to ourselves. Those connections are not static, but rather organic and ever-shifting. Members of the family are changing, calling for reparative ways to support connections to self and others. Enmeshment is a strong way to attempt to secure connections with others. Of course, if a family member does not experience his or her uniqueness welcomed by the group, connection to the group will be weakened. Hence, enmeshment is a bad imitation of real intimacy.

Coming out of an Enmeshed Family typically defines *belonging* as the ability to adapt, comply and defer to the beliefs and expectations of the group we are entering. This is an extremely artificial experience of belonging. Genuine belonging calls for the authentic desires and beliefs of the individual to be accepted and honored by the group. It means Enmeshed Family members will need to find the courage to declare who they are and to risk rejection when they wish to connect to the group. It will be extremely helpful to view rejection as a valued indicator of where you do not belong and to release the illusion that you belong everywhere.

A Blessing for Choosing Yourself

So, an enmeshed mandate had you choosing others,
remaining sensitive to what others needed.
You know how to lean into others, with care and encouragement.
Now, with a little more boundary, you learn to choose yourself.
Indictments of alleged selfishness peel away.
You're learning to honor your heart's desire.
The split between you and others fades.
As you have more of yourself, you have more to offer others.

Chapter 3

An Estranged Family or Not Enough Family

"I was so scared about being discovered, but nobody came. Nobody heard. In my own ears, though, my sobs sounded primal and scary, like something I would have turned off if I'd been able to."

- Sarah Dessen -

An Estranged Family prioritizes the autonomy and individuality of each member at the cost of sacrificing emotional connection to one another. Like all groups and communities, an Estranged Family is attempting to cope with the tension between honoring individual preferences and beliefs and uniting around a particular vision and set of values. The system operates with heavy non-permeable boundaries aimed at keeping family members separate, with the hope of minimizing disruptive behavior. The goal is to live and let live, limiting mutual support.

Parents of an Estranged Family may have been reared in an Estranged Family and are simply reproducing where they come from or compensating for the loss of individuality they experienced while being raised in an Enmeshed Family. They also may have experienced chronic trauma as children, locking them into the employment of heavy emotional and physical boundaries to feel safe.

Let's look more closely at some of the characteristics of an Estranged Family and the impact of having been raised in such a system:

Members can't depend upon receiving support from family members. The loss of family support tends to result in members becoming compulsively self-reliant. The children learn that the family is not a place to get personal needs met. Consequently, they will either learn to become very independent and/or hang out more at the homes of their friends.

Parentification. Children compensate for the lack of parenting they receive by attempting to parent themselves. This might look like the child possessing the freedom and responsibility to decide when to go to bed, whether to study, what to eat, what to wear, whom to befriend, and what to deem important. Because a child may not be ready to make sound decisions, self-sabotage becomes likely.

Family members don't really know one another. Due to the separation created by large boundaries family members don't really know each other. Not knowing people you're allegedly close to easily begins to feel familiar. It becomes easy to expect others to be anonymous and naturally inhibit disclosing who we really are. Consequently, there can be significant confusion about how to learn to trust, be trustworthy, and to distrust, as well as how to develop a meaningful rapport.

Love is defined as honoring one's own unique path and that of others. With enough inner strength and a sense of agency, children from estranged families will discover and steward their natural gifts and talents. However, accessing others as valued resources as well as seeing oneself as a valued resource for others can remain obtuse. The connective tissue to others remains mercurial and translucent. The dynamics of wanting from another and being the recipient of another's care and desire seem to remain just beyond one's reach.

Conflicts typically do not reach a resolution. Unlike an Enmeshed Family that avoids conflict, members of an Estranged Family will engage in conflict. However, there is regularly not enough empathy felt nor a desire for both parties to get their needs met to reach a resolution. Consequently, participants in the conflict are comfortable with someone feeling like they won, someone lost, or someone is right with someone else being wrong.

Members employ heavy non-permeable boundaries. This type of boundary is designed to limit the psychological material that flows from person to person. Family members are encouraged to work out their beliefs, decisions, and especially their emotions on their own. The family mandate is "don't ask, don't tell, and go take care of yourself."

Emotional intimacy remains a foreign experience. If we think of emotional intimacy as the unity of two separate unique individuals, it becomes clear why members of an Estranged Family will struggle to live intimately. The skills needed to create unity are neither modeled nor encouraged. Unlike members of an Enmeshed Family who sacrifice their uniqueness, members of an Estranged Family understand love as leaving people alone to do their own unique thing.

Compromised collaborative problem-solving. Estranged Families foster a strong "I'll have to do it myself" attitude. Because self-reliance is held as such a cherished value, family members are challenged regarding holding a vision of authentic collaboration. It may even be problematic to acknowledge needing help or asking for help. It can also be difficult to imagine someone gladly contributing to our efforts and joyfully collaborating with us.

Suggestions for Healing

It is important to remember that there are no perfect families. If you were raised in an Estranged Family as opposed to an Enmeshed Family, you can begin to calibrate just how estranged the family was. It may have been lightly estranged, moderately estranged, or heavily estranged. The more you can open to the level of estrangement you come from without catastrophizing it, the more you will be able to bring healing to your family of origin experience.

Here are some suggestions for approaching the healing process:

Getting the right help. It can be challenging to identify the loss of something we never had. Consequently, it may be important to access a psychotherapist or mentor who is familiar with the relational losses experienced in an Estranged Family. The helper needs to know how to build solid rapport so that you don't simply reproduce the estrangement you come from with the person trying to help you.

Grieving the losses related to familial disconnection. It is important to begin to experience the support of the helper by understanding what is being offered to you in the way of support and noticing what it feels like to receive it. Just such an experience can introduce you to what you did not get in childhood from family. The hope is with such an ally you can begin to feel specific losses such as being witnessed and welcomed for your accomplishments, your joy, your struggles, your sadness, your fears, and your needs and desires. You may be able to feel the loss of someone missing you and delighting in your company.

Learning how to live with semi-permeable boundaries. Typically, coming out of an Estranged Family where the norm was the use of non-permeable boundaries will likely be reproduced in adulthood. You will need to learn about the use of non-permeable boundaries in support of safety as a steady diet, since thet can create unnecessary distance. Semi-permeable boundaries are created using discriminating discernment. The goal is to both support yourself while allowing those you trust or want to get to know, to move into psychological proximity to you.

Redoing an understanding of love. This new version of love needs to include what it means to co-create a life together, how to be attuned to one another, how to name and present emotional needs to one another, remaining curious about one another, being committed to forgiving one another, creating a shared vision of what truly matters, engaging in interdependence and engaging in collective decision-making,

Learning to bring resolution to the conflict. As mentioned earlier, members of Estranged Families are not conflict-averse, they simply do not know how to reach a resolution. Foremost, there is a call to truly listen to the other without interpretations or editorial input. This is followed by an understanding of the importance to interrupt a need to either win or be right. A level of mindfulness that supports letting go of an attachment to win or be right means being willing to learn to have conversations involving diverse views and feeling the emotions that arise, while allowing for mutual curiosity about the other's position. It also entails exercising an earnest commitment to brainstorming solutions such that both parties can get their differing needs met.

Gaining emotional intimacy skills. Emotional intimacy is the real medicine for bringing healing to estrangement. When raised in an Estranged Family, it is natural to repress emotional needs. Children understand rather quickly that if they feel and acknowledge emotional needs, then they will feel alone. This alone feeling for children gets too close to be feeling there's a threat to survival. It's just much easier to deny all emotional needs, simply pretending they don't exist. Hence, the beginning place for engendering emotional intimacy is to resurrect emotional needs, being able to feel them, name them and ask for support of them.

Some examples of emotional needs include needing to be heard, seen, encouraged, nurtured, touched, acknowledged, remembered, and accompanied. We can begin building emotional intimacy when we know what to ask for and what is being emotionally asked of us. It certainly calls for remaining an apprentice of semi-permeable boundaries. The goal of such boundaries is to support our individual uniqueness while remaining accessible to others.

It also calls for understanding which of the 3 primary defenses we employ for protection: **distancing**, **dominating**, and **adapting**. We carry all three and prioritize one. Typically, too much distancing and dominating result in the loss of the other, while too much adaption leads to a loss of self. The use of these defenses can be mitigated using semi-permeable boundaries. There is also the need to learn to bring vulnerable self-disclosure into the conversation, such as expressing feeling hurt or forgotten. It is important to learn how to make clear, concrete requests of one another with all requests being legitimate. The recipient of the request has the right to respond with "No," "Yes," or "I want to negotiate." Emotional intimacy calls for raising our consciousness about how **emotional generosity** deepens our connections to each other.

The single most challenging dynamic for a family is how to support connections to others while not injuriously sacrificing connection to ourselves. Only too often in families, as well as in all kinds of configurations of relationships, the participants don't know how to hold the polarity of **self-care & relationship care**. The confusion about how to carry this polarity often leads to the participants simply prioritizing one end of the polarity while sacrificing the other side. Typically, those raised in an Enmeshed Family fear the loss of the relationship and experience abandonment fear. On the other hand, members of Estranged Families fear the loss of the self, experienced as a consumption fear.

Having experienced an Estranged Family background distorts belonging as simply the group championing the individuals to do their own thing. The missing belonging piece is the connective tissue to others. Here are some of the ways to lean into weaving connective tissue: How can we get to know each other better? Can we identify what we need and want from one another? In what ways can we be more involved in each other's life? To move in that direction means facing the fear of being consumed by others.

Knowing how to employ the right boundaries is what is needed in order to get connected to others and not consumed.

A Blessing for Choosing Others

You were offered the estranged understanding of love.
You were encouraged to choose yourself, your gifts,
your aspirations and your unique separate path.
You know how to find yourself.
Now, step into a larger love story, learning to find others.
Be curious about them.
Ask what truly matters to them, what they love,
what they fear and long for.
Be ready to say "Yes" and "No" authentically.
You won't need to be distant to feel safe.
With your "Yes" and "No" you can still choose yourself.
This act of choosing yourself and the other is messy.
Willing to stand in the mess is what is truly intimate.

Chapter 4

Perils of the Looking Good Family

"It's not the end of the physical body that should worry us. Rather, our concern must be to live while we're alive – to release our inner selves from the spiritual death that comes from living behind a façade designed to conform to external definitions of who and what we are."

- Elizabeth Kubler-Ross -

The pain in a Looking Good Family is muted behind a veil of appropriate psychological decorum. This configuration of the family runs the highest risk of living in the delusion of a perfect family. Language spoken is uplifting, designed to reference what is jovial, accomplished, and radiant. Common discourse is tightly woven with hyperbole: "That's perfect!", "Absolutely right on!", "Just wonderful!", "Couldn't be better!", "That's magnificent!", "Absolutely beautiful!", "It's just right!" Verbal embellishments are typically accompanied by lavish compliments issued to non-family members. Recipients of such endorsements are supposed to remember by whom they got their egos massaged. If it's classy and supports image, then it's a fitting protocol for the Looking Good Family.

Let's look more closely at some of the inherent dysfunctional characteristics of this family system:

Augmenting image is prioritized. The family mandate is to do whatever it takes to promote the family's image. Hobbies, education, jobs, friends and lovers, clothing, and automobiles all need to contribute appropriately to how the family is portrayed.

Moratorium on authenticity. The message to family members is: "If you have feelings, beliefs or aspirations that do not favorably contribute to the family's image, do what you need to do in order to get rid of them." Authenticity is at least implicitly shamed.

Repression of emotion. Emotions that threaten image are strongly discouraged. Anger, disgust, despair, vulnerability, bitterness, and cynicism, etc. are all taboo. The natural consequence is that coping effectively with emotions is compromised. This can yield states of depression, often accompanied by reliance upon prescription drugs, street drugs and/or alcohol.

Secrecy is valued. When family dynamics are obviously deteriorating, keeping them a secret from non-family members is strongly encouraged.

Enmeshment with poor boundaries. To preserve the likelihood of maintaining the chosen image, family members are encouraged to comply with the prevailing values and beliefs. Individual preferences and opinions are discouraged as they run the risk of threatening the prescribed image.

Denial of dysfunctional dynamics. Family members are encouraged to deny whatever dysfunctional patterns obviously detract from the desired depiction of family life. Conflicts, emotional struggles, failures, poor decisions, and a lack of cooperation should be ignored.

Impact Upon Adult Children

There are several serious repercussions involving those reared in a Looking Good Family:

The first consequence is about the child who makes a significant buy-in regarding the family's imperative to look good. The child's compliance with prioritizing image will at least periodically create identity confusion, as he or she experiences the incongruence between image and genuineness. The compliant child typically becomes perfectionistic, striving to maintain and improve upon an idyllic image. Perfectionism guarantees a gnawing feeling of inadequacy. There can also be a strong attachment to vanity.

The second reaction is an attempt to move toward something real. It can set off a protest of the looking good script. The protest can be negligible such as hairstyle or attire. However, it can also reflect an entire lifestyle, including criminal behavior and prison time. This latter act of dissent can be seriously self-sabotaging, with the adult-child never realizing that the behavior is a loud rejection of the norms of a looking good family.

Another unconscious response can be conversion reactions, which happen as repressed emotional energy manifest as undiagnosed physical symptoms. This condition is usually due to internalizing anger and stress.

Adult children often experience confusion about image vs. reality. Even if they get clear about the dysfunction in their own families, discerning image from reality remains challenging. They can easily believe that the images presented by other families reflect the reality of those families.

There is often confusion about reliable criteria for choosing friends and life partners. The puzzlement in this area reflects a significant level of distortion about image vs. authenticity. Hence, there is limited discernment available for distinguishing persona or image from who the person actually is.

Anxiety and stress usually result from attempting to sustain an idyllic image.

The Healing of Looking Good

The healing challenge is to learn to let go of allegedly unblemished perceptions of life, as well as family and self, learning to accept the flawed nature of the human condition.

There are several helpful steps in the healing process:

- Beginning to grasp that the healing process is not about moving from being exceptional to being damaged. Rather, it is transitional from what is fictional to what is authentically human.
- Generating acceptance that there is no one to blame. It is valuable to increase an understanding that the looking good dynamic is likely reflective of a family legacy. And as such, was a compensation for feeling inadequate and inferior.
- Uncoupling repression of emotion from the idea that repression is normal, so we do not continue to believe that an impoverished emotional life is normal. The key is to normalize a full range of emotional experiences.
- De-shaming authenticity. This begins by seeing the act of prioritizing image over authenticity as a wound, and likely a compensation for feelings of inadequacy. Lastly, telling the story of how we shamed being authentic. Making sure we tell the story to people we trust.
- Developing a greater capacity for discernment that helps distinguish image from reality when choosing friends and life partners. Some discerning questions

include: Does this person know what brings meaning to his or her life? Is this person curious about what brings meaning to my life? Are they capable of being honest about limits, regrets, and shortcomings? Do they live with gratitude? Are they materially and emotionally generous? Can they appreciate diverse views and perspectives?

- Learning to develop rapport with others by being honest and compassionate rather than by being impressive or fabricating inflated compliments.

My experience is that healing does not necessarily come easy for members of a Looking Good Family. There is an assemblage of delusion to wade through, and that can be quite challenging to the loyalty of someone raised in such a system. Let's look at the responses of two people beginning to explore their looking good beginnings.

The first is Daniel, a 55-old chemical engineer, married with three adult children. During his first appointment with me, he made it clear that he wasn't sure why he was in my office.

"Well, I guess I'm here because my wife really wants me to be. I mean, I like my life, my job, my home, and my marriage is probably as good as it gets," Daniel offered, with concentrated eye contact, not suggestive of rapport building, but more of an intensity encouraging my agreement.

"Daniel, I'm open to exploring if there is some way I can help you, but I don't hear that there is some area of your life that you want help to examine," I pointed out, hoping he might be willing to allow me to join him in an honest inventory of life, rather than simply satisfying his spouse's investment in his therapy.

"I don't want to waste your time and mine. My wife thinks I have an emotional problem. She thinks it comes from my upbringing, which I have difficulty believing. I mean, I come from a wonderful family. My folks stayed together, there were never any fights, we all went to church every Sunday, as kids we did well in school, the boys played sports, the girls took dance classes and we all ended up with pretty good jobs," Daniel reported, not attempting to diminish any of the idyllic tones of his account.

"Wow, it does sound like a good family situation. Did you ever witness anyone crying or cussing?" I asked, wondering how accepting the system was regarding the expression of emotion.

"I remember my little sister crying once when she got soap in her eyes during a bath. I don't think there was anything really to cry about. And why would someone cuss? Life was terrific. There was no real reason to get upset. People smiled a lot," Daniel added, very willing to continue sanitizing family life to explain the non-existence of emotion.

"I see. People smiled a lot. You never saw a family member depressed, confused, disappointed, or scared?" I probed, wondering if he recalled any expression of emotion.

"I imagine that people felt some of those things, but nobody ever showed it. I mean why would you want someone to see you like that? What's so great about that?" he maintained, possibly revealing a family norm to keep your emotions to yourself.

"Sometimes, families offer support to one another during difficult times. They encourage each member to express what they are feeling and get help," I pointed out, wondering if he might be able to see another option to family life.

"I guess those would be really troubled families. There was no trouble in our family. People didn't need help. I know it sounds strange, but I was raised in a perfect family," Daniel claimed, with the tacit suggestion that it was just inconceivable that one could not get how unblemished his family of origin was.

Daniel was not about to betray the alleged refinement of his family. It wasn't until his aging parents began to be enthralled with conservative politics, that he began to wonder what their values really were. I decided to introduce him to the characteristics of the Looking Good Family, including ideology that is framed in black and white thinking. To which he responded, "They did appreciate thinking that lacked ambiguity." Luckily, due to the commitment to his marriage, Daniel continues to examine where he came from, easing into the truth about the values, the expectations, and the taboos of his family of origin. He often discloses, "I just don't know how much was real back then," easing through copious levels of delusion.

Amanda, a 48-year-old female social worker came in to see me, wanting to look more closely at her family of origin. She was clear about having been raised in an alcoholic family and she had been participating in a 12 Step Program for a number of years to help her understand them. I sensed she was ready to take a closer look at where she came from. After identifying a strong level of enmeshment in her family of origin, I decided to offer her some information about the Looking Good Family. She came to her following session with noticeable relief.

"I can't believe how much the material on the Looking Good Family so clearly outlined where I come from! There was ongoing chaos in the home. My brother acted out constantly, my parents, both alcoholics, bickered daily and we weren't allowed to talk about any of it. Amid the chaos, you weren't supposed to blow your nose, cry, or have a menstrual period. It was like all bodily secretions were taboo. What really mattered was how you looked as you prepared to leave the home," Amanda was moving through the delusions spawned by her family, and in doing so, she was welcoming her own humanity with more acceptance.

She went on to describe how visits to her friend Carol's house began opening her eyes to the well-constructed facade of her family. As a teenager, she took the risk of letting Carol know what went on behind the scenes in her home. It also helped when Carol confirmed that what Amanda witnessed in her home was what went on when Amanda wasn't visiting. All of which went a long way to support Amanda's clarity about her Looking Good Family.

Daniel and Amanda represent the different levels of readiness to let go of any illusions of having come from a perfect family. Even though Amanda's parents insidiously suggested that the family chaos was simply how well-balanced families interact, Amanda had enough personal work to tug on the looking good veil. While the repression of all emotion may have made it more difficult for Daniel to see the denunciation of authenticity which marked the culture of his family.

It may be that the authentic life is never easily attained or even desired. It means we need to get straight with ourselves, learning to welcome less than exemplary qualities. Envy, arrogance, lethargy, and vanity are typically exiled by the average ego. Once we are willing to drop the denial of these indigent parts of ourselves, the door opens to the genuine self, accompanied by a new depth of freedom. Our psychological task is to begin understanding how these darker elements helped us to negotiate an insecure and unpredictable journey. From such understanding, the buds of compassion may sprout, yielding a bountiful welcome to a larger self, finding its place in the human condition. Genuine acceptance of who we are takes the place of looking good.

Being raised in the Looking Good Family seriously skews the experience of genuine belonging, since the parents were heavily externally referenced, adapting prevailing political, religious, and social conventions. There is nothing real in the family. In order to explore genuine belonging, individuals will need to betray the system by denying it's alleged perfection. Then, take on the task of becoming more internally referenced: "I know such and such is quite popular, but what are my real feelings, beliefs and values?" From this internally referenced place, survivors of Looking Good Families can at least explore the possibility of belonging, by identifying and speaking their personal truths, especially those that might be described as more creaturely. These may include a hunger for food, touch, and affiliation; feeling sad, angry, scared, and lost; feeling tired or ill.

A Blessing for Getting Real

It is an arduous journey to hold loyalty to those
holding tight to illusion.
Your parents likely could no longer bear the weight of their shame,
with no relief offered by reality.
Hence, the attachment to a chimera created by what the
culture deemed appropriate.
In that acculturation, soul is lost, in its place a duplicitous
map guiding how to think, act, dress, and work.
And then the slickest of all conjuring.
Since our choices are all lined up with the prevailing cultural
prescriptions, we must be the perfect family.
Slowly, come to know the quiet voice within you,
the voice making it okay to be not okay.
You will hear sadness, anger, desperation, fear, joy and hurt.
Feel the perspiration on a body that wants to move,
rest and be held.
What looks good begins to fade with the soul of your humanity
taking its rightful place.

Chapter 5

The Shame-Based Family

"We live in a world where most people still subscribe to the belief that shame is a good tool for keeping people in line. Not only is this wrong, but it's dangerous. Shame is highly correlated with addiction, violence, aggression, depression, eating disorders, and bullying."

- Brene Brown -

We all know the dreadful and debilitating feeling of "There's something terribly wrong here, and the something is me!" Although far from enjoyable, or welcomed, such a feeling can be helpful. For example, if you act contrary to your integrity, violating one of your core values, what has been described as "healthy shame" can be a wake-up call, summoning you back to yourself. When accompanied by self-forgiveness, healthy shame does not turn us against ourselves. Rather, it points to what it means to get right with ourselves. In fact, parents who model healthy shame offer their children an inextricable depiction of living in integrity and exercising self-accountability.

Parental Modeling of Shame

According to John Bradshaw, "Toxic shame, the shame that binds you, is experienced as the all-pervasive sense that I am flawed and defective as a human being." There are several ways in which shame becomes galvanized in the family system. This results in its members becoming over-identified with feeling shame.

If parents are living with shame at the core of their identities, then children can easily adopt the modeling and feel the grip of shame. Jack and his wife, Maryann, came in to see me, reporting their concerns about their children.

"We have worked very hard at not shaming our children. We practice self-accountability, promoting acceptance of all emotions, and we exercise logical and concrete consequences to address unacceptable behavior. I think we're doing a great job," Maryann noted, her tone carrying the enthusiasm and conviction of someone giving a lecture on proper parenting. It left me wondering what the driving force behind her zeal might be.

"Maryann, I'm hearing that you and Jack have really done your homework as parents. Tell me more about what brings you here," I encouraged, feeling her readiness to reveal more.

"Well, it's our kids. If one of them makes a mistake, spills juice, forgets to take out the trash or feed the dog, their heads immediately hang in shame. And we're telling them it's perfectly okay, but it doesn't matter. They continue doing a number on themselves. I just know it's nothing we've done!" Maryann exclaimed, with her chin slightly lifted, and her eye contact darting away, as if something much more attractive got her attention.

"I think you and Jack have been doing a good job parenting. I'm more wondering about the families you both come from. Did shame ever show up at the dinner table?" I inquired, hoping they might have some understanding of their histories with shame. A shroud of silence entered the room, heavy as the early morning fog over the bay.

"Well, both of us were the objects of considerable shaming by our parents. But that's why we've been so determined not to shame our children. I mean, we know what it's like," Jack declared, leaning forward in a manner suggesting a solicitation of agreement.

"How do each of you feel when you make a mistake?" I asked, sensing it was the right question, but not knowing if I wandered down a hornet's hive of denial.

"I need to admit it. I can really beat up on myself. I guess the old shame can still have its way with me," Maryann shared, her eyes moistening and her tone suggesting defeat.

It was clear that Jack and Maryann believed that they could simply relate to their children shamelessly and shame would not take hold of their children. I went on to assure them that they were good parents. I made it clear that for the most part, only good parents find their way to my office. I went on to explain with a measure of empathy, that they were modeling what it meant to live with internalized shame. I added that the greatest gift to their children would be for them to take care of themselves. I recommended several therapists who could be helpful in their own de-shaming process. Maryann acted upon my suggestion and Jack continued to work with me. They were committed to interrupting the internalized shame they were carrying, which led to the de-shaming of their family.

Severing the "Interpersonal Bridge"

In his seminal work, *Shame: The Power of Caring*, Gershen Kaufman addresses the second way that a family becomes shame-based: "An emotional bond begins to grow between individuals as they communicate understanding, respect, and valuing for one another's personhood, needs and feelings included. That bond deepens along with trust and makes possible experiences of openness and vulnerability. The bond which ties two individuals together forms an interpersonal bridge between them. The bridge in turn becomes a vehicle to facilitate mutual understanding, growth, and change. These vital processes are disrupted whenever that bridge becomes severed." Kaufman goes on to suggest that the forces of humiliation, disgust, contempt, disparagement as well excessive expectations are what severs the "interpersonal bridge," replacing it with shame.

The Shame Collage

The third infusion of shame into the system happens by way of what Bradshaw calls, in *Healing the Shame that Binds You*, "the interconnection of memory imprints which forms collages of shame." This process takes place as a particular behavior receives ongoing disparaging reactions. For example, if a child hears contemptuous overtones when asked about homework, that same child is likely to feel shame when an innocuous, non-shaming question is asked about homework. When shame is internalized, it becomes difficult to discern whether something toxic or not is heading your way. Internalized feelings of shame can easily become generalized and attached to other questions having nothing to do with homework. Children can begin to feel the shame associated with a variety of questions related to domestic chores. Now being the recipient of any inquiry can elicit shame.

Taking on the Shame of a Perpetrator

The fourth inculcation of shame can happen when a child is physically or sexually abused, and the perpetrator takes no accountability for the violation. A child easily determines that something unacceptable has occurred and yet the perpetrator has not taken responsibility for acting abusively. Victims step into the vacuum of accountability and decide they must be responsible for such a reprehensible act. Such a decision is commonly accompanied by feeling shame.

Characteristics of a Shame-Based Family

We've been examining the ways shame gets instilled into a family. Let's look more closely at some of the characteristics of a shame-based family:

Parents have internalized shame. Inevitably, the leaders or parents will be carrying internalized shame. When that happens, unlike Jack and Maryann, the parents will be both modeling living in shame as well as verbally and non-verbally shaming the children. Each family member will be a stranger to feeling okay about themselves, not having a genuine felt sense of their essential worth as human beings.

The family mandate. The mandate of the shame-based family is the contemptible self must remain hidden. Fear drives this imperative to safeguard against others, witnessing how truly unlovable family members are. The fear condemns everyone to live with an inconsolable feeling of vulnerability.

Developing a false self. With the actual self becoming a fugitive sequestered to some undisclosed chamber of the psyche, a false self is fashioned for worldly encounters. This imitation of the self is limited to *pleasing, impressing, avoiding,* and *dominating*. The job of the false self includes monitoring and inhibiting the genuine expression of emotion, desires, needs and values.

The damage of absenteeism. It's too easy to think of absent parents as simply not available physically. However, parents make a devastating declaration when they announce that their genuine selves will not be available. When children can't fine the authentic self of a parent, they are not able to create what Kaufman referred to as the "interpersonal bridge." That is, they cannot create "a vehicle to facilitate mutual understanding, growth, and change." When the bridge cannot be constructed, children face life with an insurmountable level of insecurity and instability. They no longer feel safe and likely feel abandoned. They will likely require similar restorative therapeutic support as children whose parents stepped out of their lives. They attach the best they can to the parent's false self, leaving themselves with a significantly compromised psychological scaffolding.

Becoming externally referenced. When family members are convinced that they do not possess the internal resources needed to engender something redemptive, they wait for something from the external world to save them. Someone might want to date them, hire them, include them, befriend them, or even marry them. However, their longings are of no avail, for even if love is coming to them, they can find ways to disqualify the offering, like "the person doesn't really know me" or "there must be someone who would be a better fit for me." It can be an arduous journey before they discover they are the only ones who can restore their essential goodness.

Developing compensations. The ego naturally attempts to compensate for shame's sting of feeling worthless. One form of compensation is perfectionism which does not possess the power to lift a person out of the depths of self-loathing. Compulsive caregiving is another compensation, in the hope that someone will validate one's elusive credibility as a good person. Sometimes, a compensation shows up as excessive striving as deservedness is allegedly measured by copious levels of exertion. "I must be okay; look how hard I'm trying." Another compensation is self-righteousness, a flawed attempt to restore a longing for feeling acceptable.

No-talk rule. Once the false self of parents is allegedly in charge, members of the family feel increasingly out of control.

An imperative to suppress the expression of honest emotion, desires, needs and occasionally actual family rules dictates how people relate. It's an erroneous strategy aimed at restoring some measure of stability to the system.

Boundary violation. Once the "interpersonal bridge" has been severed, empathy in the system atrophies. Family members suspend monitoring what they say to one another. With emotional boundaries being easily violated, respect for individual preferences and needs withers. Withdrawal and avoidance are employed as boundaries causing an enhanced level of estrangement.

Anger. Anger is the only emotion tolerated. It can be used as a boundary, pushing people away. It is typically employed as a strategy to move away from feeling vulnerable. It's not unusual for family members to express more anger as they increasingly feel more vulnerable.

Repairing 2 Bridges

It is important to understand that healing is very available for those raised in a Shame-Based family. Essentially, it means repairing the bridge to the authentic self as well as the bridge to trusted others.

Repairing the Bridge to the Authentic Self

Let's look more closely at the psychological infrastructure supporting repair:

Psychological education. Coming to understand that your family of origin was not what you may have thought of as normal, but was rather shame based. Hence, you are not damaged goods, but you are likely continuing to carry several psychological patterns learned in your family. While growing up in that family, there was no way to know and feel your essential worth as a human being.

Developing an interior welcoming. Learning to shamelessly welcome your emotions, desires and needs is a crucial pillar in the reconstruction of this first bridge. Initially, it is just about letting yourself be aware of who you are emotionally. Your acquaintance with your emotions strengthens as you develop a felt sense of them in your body. This experience could be fear felt as butterflies in the belly, sadness expressed as heaviness in the chest, or anger reflected by tightness in the shoulders and jaw. Personal power unfolds as you offer an earnest greeting to the more vulnerable aspects such as hurt and fear. What can occur in your interior world may reflect what happens in the external world. For example, we know that a society is as strong as its capacity to integrate its most vulnerable members - children, the elderly, the disabled - as well as remaining open to who may feel marginalized. So, it is in the internal world. As the more vulnerable parts of the self are assimilated, a robustness will be restored to your sense of being, known as personal power.

Opportunity to grieve. As you open to your emotions, it can be a time to grieve the losses of the past. Don't do this alone. At least sit with one trusted person who understands what it means to address loss. Your losses will include feeling understood, feeling loved and accepted, feeling secure and safe, being comfortable making mistakes as well as being a recipient of kindness.

Interrupting shaming voices. Most of the shaming voices you carry don't belong to you. It's likely they are introjected from the past. This means you internalized parental shaming directed at you. You can stop talking to yourself the way your parents addressed you. Practice holding the message, "That's not my voice and what it says about me is not true."

Giving shame back. You did not emerge from the womb believing there was something wrong with you. The shame you carry doesn't belong to you. You can write a letter to your parents that you don't necessarily intend to send. In the letter describe the toxic accusations that were hurled at you. Let the parent know those indictments don't belong to you and you're giving them back.

Make peace with being imperfect. In a system where there is ongoing assault on your strengths and weaknesses, honoring your imperfect humanity is almost impossible. It is only too easy to believe everyone else is fine and that the gods simply forgot to furnish you with desirable attributes. Initially, defining your humanity as imperfect might be baffling. One of the best ways to make peace with your imperfection is to apprentice to making mistakes compassionately. Allow one mistake at a time to be a statement of your humanity and not your flawed character.

Shamelessly accountable. A shame-based family merges shame with accountability. Hence, if you're accountable for some action then you are the deplorable person who blundered. It is a spiritual practice to de-shame accountability. The new mantra sounds like, "I am the good person who is accountable for my mistakes. Being accountable means that I acknowledge what I did. I make restitution whenever possible. I only feel healthy shame when I violate one of my core values."

Building self-trust. You learned in your family not to trust yourself. Why would you ever think of trusting a defective human being? Besides, not trusting yourself helped to deter you from saying or doing things that could easily leave you vulnerable to toxic scrutiny. As you can recall that your perceptions of yourself have been unscrupulously distorted by the system you come from, you can begin to hold that you are trustworthy. Trust for yourself begins to build as you engender two beliefs: first, you believe you will allow yourself to know your truth without self-incrimination. Your truth is your emotions, your desires, and needs, as well as your beliefs and values. Secondly, you come to believe you will be kind to yourself. Kindness is a measure of interrupting self-shaming thoughts as well as behaviors not contributing to your general welfare.

Repairing abandonment trauma. This trauma configures around the belief that you were abandoned or forgotten because you are not worthy of being remembered. This belief is typically accompanied by despair, anguish, and the loss of faith that being loved is possible, as well as an unregulated nervous system. I highly recommend somatic therapeutic interventions such as EMDR and Somatic Experiencing. As this repair strengthens, the initial belief explaining how you were forgotten is replaced by **"I was forgotten by my parents because they did not know how to remember themselves."** I highly recommend working with a practitioner well-acquainted with the power and healing potential of the above statement.

Reparenting yourself. We normally think of abandonment as taking place between two people. However, survivors of Shamed-Based Families easily get caught up in a torrid stream of self-abandonment. They forget themselves as they were forgotten. They forget to encourage themselves, forget to eat, rest, play and access the support of a friend. A key is to remember the vulnerable child who was shamed and who is still with you. These psychological parts of ourselves don't go away or die. I recommend the use of my **BEND** model for reparenting yourself. You can give yourself a new parent by adopting the skills suggested by the acronym. **"B" stands for effective Boundaries**. These should be strong enough to supply protection and porous enough to let love in. **"E" refers to Encouragement.** Let your inner child know you believe in him or her and that they are well worth your attention. **"N" denotes Nurturing**. Come to know what truly nurtures you - walks in the forest, playing, hot baths, being held, coffee with a friend or a day at the beach. **"D" stands for Discipline**. Here, I draw from an ancient definition of the word *discipline,* which is "discipleship." Hence, come to know your allies, those trusted others who are committed to knowing you, loving you and believing in you. Call them in for help and support whether the task be something custodial or emotional.

Repairing the Bridge to Others

As you learn to build bridges to trusted others, remain mindful of a prevalent cultural seduction. This temptation comes in the way of an extroverted culture's infatuation with flares of exuberance, suggesting the alleged presence of a meaningful human encounter. That's not to say demonstrations of jubilation cannot create bonding. It is just that the relational story is larger. We begin with the question, what constitutes the refined material needed for a sturdy "interpersonal bridge"?

The refined material. The refined material for the bridge to others is the bridge to yourself. The only thing in your control when encountering others is the connection to the authentic self. Relating to others meaningfully is not mostly about being with them, it is mostly about being with yourself in their presence. The more you trust yourself, the more discernment you bring to allowing your truth to come forward. Building a bridge to the authentic self is the prerequisite to all relationship building.

Mindful of the false self. Pleasing, impressing, avoiding, and dominating are natural expressions of the false self. We do these to support our survival, which gets amplified in a shame-based family. The key is not to make a big deal about these fabricated expressions of the self. Simply, get to know when they are present and decide to go with it or let it go. It's important to appreciate how much the expressions of the false self have served you, exercise them now with more intention when you need one. Recently, a relatively new friend turned to me at a dinner party and said, "I've been noticing my attachment to impressing you," as a glow of shyness shown in her rosy cheeks. I felt gifted and thankful to receive her truth, which eclipsed her false self. You don't need years of psychotherapy to cope effectively with the faces of the false self. It does call for a willingness to risk while refusing to shame the outcome.

Building trust for others. Trust must be earned. I recently heard a gentleman proudly declare his willingness to trust whoever shows up in his life. I suggested he may not be doing anyone a favor by trusting without discernment.

"Do you believe that it makes a favorable statement about you that you're so willing to magnanimously offer your trust?" I asked, noticing a glimmer of pride reflected off his face.

"Well, I'm at least giving people a chance," he offered, attempting to build a case for the viability of his approach toward trust.

"Actually, I believe you can give people a chance without quickly deciding they deserve your trust. You can remain observant without drawing quick conclusions, allowing for an informed expression of discernment. Without discernment, there's a risk of setting people up to fail, not being deserving of your trust while making you unnecessarily vulnerable to being hurt," I explained, wondering if he would be willing to loosen his grip upon the alleged meritorious act of trusting without discretion.

"You make it sound like distrust is some good thing!" he

exclaimed, his lips tightening, his brow furrowing, and eyes squinting, suggesting he was hearing the unbelievable.

"Of course, it's a good thing. If someone demonstrates a tendency to lie to you or be consistently unkind, then you should distrust them," I offered, wondering if Frank might open to a new perspective.

"Okay, I think I hear what you're saying. People gain my trust when I have enough experience with them, I have some experience hearing them telling me the truth and being kind to me," he responded, with his gaze softening and his torso leaning forward.

"That's right, giving yourself time to gather enough information to make something approaching an informed decision. You can still be the guy who enjoys trusting, but doing it because the person has earned it," I encouraged, hoping he could see it wasn't necessary for him to sacrifice his love of trusting.

"How do I know how much time to give someone before I make a decision?" he asked, his desire to understand being palpable.

"Frank, that's a great question. One approach is to pay attention to what impresses you and what turns you off when you meet people. If you're easily impressed by beauty, intelligence, social status, or charisma, then slow down the process of trusting. You'll run the risk of trusting a bit too quickly. If you're turned off by someone's accent, type of work, or where they live, then slow down your distrust. You may be distrusting too hastily," I rejoined, in the hope that Frank could see what might influence his offerings of trust.

Remaining a student of effective boundaries. A verbal or physical boundary is what you do to separate yourself from another. Purposeful separation might be safety or to confirm your unique needs or views. The degree to which a boundary provides a level of separation is one way to understand them. Permeable boundaries allow for very little separation, while non-permeable ones furnish a great deal of separation. Semi-permeable boundaries provide a fluid level of separation depending upon how much separation is needed. These boundaries are adjusted to be more permeable when you're in the presence of what is benign, acceptable, or valued, such as offerings of kindness, support, and love. They can be modified to be more non-permeable when encountering what is deemed as threatening, harsh, or unacceptable - such as sarcasm, ridicule, or shame. Regulation of semi-permeable boundaries is accomplished by exercising discernment, which is guided by a quality of self-trust. The more you trust yourself, the greater the likelihood that your discernment will reveal what's nefarious and what's favorable. Becoming skillful with the employment of semi-permeable boundaries is very advantageous because they allow you to benefit from what is loving and kind and to protect you from what may be toxic. Shame-Based Families tend to operate with very permeable boundaries within the system and amongst its members, who get to say and do whatever moves them, often flaunting a cavalier attitude about being unkind. However, because of the shame and vulnerability experienced by family members, non-permeable boundaries are employed when encountering anyone outside the family.

Getting Messy. Survivors of Shame-Based Families rely upon shame to cope with relationships when then get messy, resulting in things getting messier. The messy ingredients may include someone feeling hurt, scared, forgotten or angry. Relationships also get messy when there is some form of conflict. Messy happens when people feel lost and bewildered or when any level of meaningful change is occurring, even events like marriages and funerals. When something messy shows up, what sits just beneath the shame is fear. Again, we see the importance of the bridge to the authentic self as we construct a bridge to others. Survivors will need to increase their ability to feel fear, acknowledge fear and calm themselves to effectively deal with what is messy.

Being adept at both speaking and listening to the fear of others calls for an aptitude for holding tension. We can say that the hallmark of coping with messy is being able to hold tension without resorting to utterances of shame. I recommend several steps regarding holding tension. First, notice where the tension sits in your body. Secondly, bring your breath to where the tension sits and remain focused upon that area. If it feels right, verbally acknowledge the tension to a trusted other. If you find you're getting a bit immobilized, then move your fingers and hands gently or get up and take a walk. The frozen reaction occurs because what's happening is a reminder of some historical messy situation accompanied by shaming. Use your eyes for grounding by simply looking around the room at different objects.

Getting messy with relational breakdowns. Building bridges to others certainly happens when we are attuned to them and experience genuine resonance. Being attuned means that we are letting go of whatever has our attention and tuning in to what the other is presenting to us. It may be an idea, an emotion, or some desire. Resonance occurs as the emotions of two people come into sync, reflecting and encouraging of one another's emotional state. Conflicts and other forms of relational breakdowns are what's messy when trying to build "interpersonal bridges." When we experience relational breakdowns with no resolution and are left feeling accused and blamed, we lose faith that attunement and resonance are even possible. One way to attend to the messiness of relational breakdowns is to adopt a protocol called problem ownership. Unfortunately, in a Shame-Based Family, problem disownership is the norm. That is, whenever someone has a problem, they hand it off to another family member via accusation, blame or ridicule. Some years ago, pioneers in the Human Potential movement, like Thomas Gordon, took the issue of problem disownership quite seriously. These trailblazers decided that the relational mess gets out of hand because there is no clarity about the actual problem and who has it. **They decided that in many cases, the real problem is an unmet need; and the person with the problem is the person with the unmet need**. A simple emotional review easily reveals who has the unmet need. It is the person talking about needing or wanting something and have feelings like frustration, anger, and discouragement because the need is not being met. Of course, if we speak in code, suggesting that the problem is the other's insensitivity, carelessness, and non-cooperative behavior, then it is more challenging to identify the real problem and who has it. Messiness becomes a bit less messy if two people can buy in on problem ownership.

Those of us raised in Shame-Based Families can, with help, restore a connection to our essential goodness. You are not basically flawed! You've been living in a shame story whose narrative can be redeemed. You will likely need to give back the shame that doesn't belong to you. Parents who feel out of control often resort to shame in a desperate attempt to control their children. As parents live with their own unaddressed shame, children can easily shame themselves due to the modeling.

Do what you can to interact with people who do not relate to themselves or others with the arbitrary use of shame. You may even ascribe fraudulence when encountering compassion, authenticity, gentleness, and acceptance. Just notice your suspicions and continue to spend time where these new energies appear to thrive. Exercise your discernment, no one will be perfectly gentle or compassionate. You will eventually discover whether the actions you witness are either genuine or pretentious.

Genuine belonging coming out of a Shame-Based Family is very challenging. The issue is how deeply vulnerable folks feel due to the bite of shame. They can't imagine their unique selves being worthy of acceptance and invitations from others. The first step is to give back the shame to those who shamed you. The second step is to begin gradually building a shameless belonging with yourself. This is initiated by interrupting critical and derogatory descriptions of your choices and behaviors. It is important that your sense of belonging begin with your relationship with yourself. With good therapeutic support, your essential worth can be recovered, engendering the belief that others can and will appreciate who you are.

A Blessing for Coming Out of the Shadows

Living in the shadows of shame can feel normal.
You don't belong there!
Your parents felt terribly out of control and desperately employed shame to regain control.
Or they brought to you their own childhood shame with them, modeling self-loathing.
You don't belong there!
Your essential goodness sits in the recesses of your psyche, waiting to be reclaimed.
Humility's voice whispers, "Learn to graciously accept your limits."
Hear the invitation to welcome the imperfection of your humanity.
Allow humility to be where you rest, relinquishing tireless efforts of striving.
Gently welcome yourself into the light of your abiding goodness.

Chapter 6

Grace and Limits for the Family Hero

"Show me a hero, and I'll write you a tragedy."

- F. Scott Fitzgerald -

There are several roles that children can take on in a family. The more stress in a family the more rigidly children cling to one role, which leaves the advantages of the other roles unavailable to them. The most popular role is identified as the Hero. Inevitably, this child will receive the most positive attention, encouragement, and praise. It is a coveted family role, often reserved for the oldest or an only child.

There are several favorable qualities associated with the Hero role. Heroes know how to read and respond to the expectations of those holding authority. They tend to be very willing to take on responsibility for a task or to take on a measured risk. Heroes are typically steadfast and reliable regarding their regular work ethic. They are often quite clear about their values and what it means to live with integrity.

However, when the role is taken on inflexibly, not refined by the features of other roles, beneficial characteristics as well as more harmful heroic tendencies can easily be carried into adulthood. These children easily become leaders and helpers, such as doctors, nurses, psychologists, social workers, clergy, teachers, consultants, and executive coaches.

Prominent Characteristics

Let's look at the characteristics of this role that need repair:

Loving and being lovable are organized and defined as achieving. The dilemma is that the Hero will feel condemned to endless manifestations of success as demonstrations of self-worth. They can't imagine someone loving them simply because of who they are, as they constantly attempt to prove they are lovable by adding to their resume.

Excessive striving. Heroes are constantly striving to get life right. This strenuous effort places a serious prohibition upon living with peace and joy. Perfectionism easily becomes a way of life. Taking up lodging in the idyllic house of perfectionism condemns the Hero to a gnawing sense of not being enough.

Have trouble feeling satisfied with their achievements. The demand for perfection won't allow for feelings of gratification and fulfillment. Living with the gravitas of severity becomes familiar with a mitigated level of joy.

Weaknesses are easily denied. Heroes can be highly attached to what I call a shiny persona, an investment in looking good. They turn to their strengths again and again. A typical strength for a Hero is intellectual acuity, which leaves their emotional intelligence ignored and underdeveloped. They easily lose sight of their developmental edge.

Compulsive self-reliance. As the need to see themselves as accomplished expands, so does the need to see receiving assistance and support from others as unnecessary. This exaggerated independence can greatly hamper a capacity for collaboration and collective problem-solving. They easily believe that if they want something to get accomplished, then they should do it themselves. It also disables an abiding ability to be relational as their independent persona leads others to believe they have nothing to offer the Hero, possessing an undeveloped capacity to receive from others.

Emotional isolation. One consequence of heroic self-reliance is the absence of genuine rapport, where they would feel known, understood, and loved. Such isolation has Heroes possessing an undeveloped capacity to receive from others, which includes a tendency to suppress their needs. If an unsuppressed need reaches the surface, then Heroes will likely view the need as an expression of failure.

Identity can be trapped in a high-achieving role. Heroes often do not know who they are beyond the scope of their professional roles. There's confusion about what they love, fear, need, and the range of their losses. Their myopic view of themselves measured by high achievement easily morphs into a haunting self-righteousness.

Easily generate the illusion that they can save others. To bolster their much-treasured self-concept as highly capable, Heroes easily come to believe they can save others. This illusion easily shifts into resentment as others appear not to respond favorably to heroic gestures of saving. Heroes can easily remain distracted by their saving efforts, thereby neglecting the only person they can truly save, themselves.

Condemned to Conditional Self-Regard. Regardless of a specific professional endeavor, Heroes tend to be relatively successful in their chosen field. Of course, a level of prosperity will likely make it easier for a Hero to remain in denial regarding anything curative being helpful. I often think of Sisyphus and Icarus as the patron saints of Heroes. Icarus and his father Daedalus are held captive in a labyrinth by King Minos.

Daedalus crafts two sets of wings made of feathers and wax which are intended to allow father and son to fly out of the labyrinth. Icarus is cautioned not to fly high, close to the sun, resulting in the wax melting and Icarus's demise, which is exactly what happens. Icarus is often viewed as a tragic figure driven by hubris which has him denying his limits and paying a lethal price. Similar to Icarus, Heroes tend to deny their limits, making them more vulnerable to stress, illness and burnout. Then there is Sisyphus who is described as the deceitful and impious king of Corinth. He was determined to escape death and be immortal, which angered the gods. He is condemned to Tartarus with the task of eternally rolling a rock up a hill only to have it roll back down and starting all over again. The story of Sisyphus can remind Heroes that they can easily condemn themselves to a perpetual need to prove and demonstrate their worthiness. Such a condemnation leaves the Hero or Heroine driven by a conditional self-acceptance. I would offer the following mantra as a reflection of the conditions: "I do a lot - I make a lot - I acquire a lot - therefore, I am a lot." Heroes may never recover the unconditional self-worth they possessed upon departure from the womb.

Healing for Heroes

More than any other family role, Heroes deny that they need help. Consequently, it can be very challenging for them to get the support that they need to outgrow the debilitating aspects of the role. However, if they can find enough humility and courage as well as a resource that is not seduced by their level of success, then the following interventions can go a long way to restore Heroes to the fullness of their humanity.

Letting go of achieving as a measure of love. Achieving condemns Heroes to conditional self-love, leaving them condemned to proving that they are okay repeatedly. They can at least approach living with unconditional self-love by committing to living with more humility. **If we understand humility as the gracious acceptance of personal limits, then Heroes can gradually shed the need to demonstrate their worth. They can live with compassion and acceptance for all of themselves, and not just the part of them who succeeds.** As a result, what makes them lovable to others is their authenticity, a capacity for compassion, generosity, and gratitude. Heroes tend to give others the power to confirm their personal value by being excessively attached to being impressive. Watching such an attachment and interrupting it is a wonderful way for Heroes to reclaim the power to confirm their own worth. A recent conversation with a recovering Hero demonstrated the spiritual practice of tracking and interrupting an attachment to being impressive. "I've been tracking my need to impress for some time. Recently, I noticed that not only do I want the listener to be impressed with my varied performances, but I also want whoever is listening to be impressed with the subtly by which I deliver my declarations." **Random acts of self-kindness can become a wonderful way to replace striving and proving**. Anything that is fun or nurturing works. Playing games that are not heavily competitive, saunas, massage, naps, sitting quietly appreciating nature, talking with an old friend, walks on a beach, watching a good movie, moving slowly from event A to event B, listening to music and dancing.

Interrupting excessive striving. As Heroes begin to accept who they are now, the need to prove their worth is mitigated, allowing for unnecessary endeavoring to subside. It becomes especially important for Heroes to learn how to reclaim a lightness of heart. Learning how to play non-competitively, taking walks with family and friends, finding permission to sing and dance, finding a way to express themselves creatively and noticing and feeling what touches and moves them emotionally.

Feeling deep satisfaction for a job well done. When Heroes begin to mitigate the quality of job performance as a measure of their personal worth, they can begin to simply feel the reward of having optimized their efforts with desired results. Much is gained by celebrating accomplishments with friends.

Carrying an internal bow of humility. Carrying the metaphor of an internal bow allows Heroes to embrace a realistic view of their humanity. The metaphor points toward what is larger than the individual Hero. It may be a support group, a team, Nature, a family, or a deity. The key is to remain in a relationship with something larger than one's ego, holding the faith that whatever is larger can provide more than an individual effort. Coming back to holding gratitude repeatedly can greatly support the connection to something larger.

Inventorying & accepting strengths and areas needing development. Heroes often know their strengths and tend either to be unconscious of or in denial about areas needing development. Shortcomings simply don't go with the role, which leaves Heroes with a skewed self-concept. At its worse, Heroes will feel shame about their limitations. It can be helpful to work closely with social practitioners, coaches, and developmental assistants to canvas areas of development repeatedly as simply ways of growing and not a self-indictment. As mentioned earlier, Heroes typically have well-developed intellects and need to pay attention to their emotional intelligence. This becomes particularly important as neuroscientists remind us that emotions have a large impact upon the formation of beliefs and ensuing actions.

Learning to empower others rather than attempting to save. Even when saving looks like it might be working, it enables the disempowerment of the person allegedly being saved. Efforts directed at saving do not affirm the competency, intelligence, and capability of people. Gestures of saving are simply displaying of the savior's prowess. There's always room for Heroes to become better listeners while helping others to identify both internal and external resources. In doing so, Heroes empower others, supporting the agency of those around them.

Leaning into unconditional self-regard. This can be an arduous task for Heroes. It will take a devotion to four steps that call for an ongoing renewal. **Step 1 – Learn to graciously accept your limits, Step 2 – Practice self-kindness, Step 3 – Practice self-forgiveness, Step 4 – Remain receptive to accepting love from those who you trust.** These steps support a deep, integrated sense of deservedness.

Hero children loved their parents by performing well academically and/or athletically. They offered their caregivers a pleasant distraction from the challenges they faced. Ultimately, these children become adults who need to reorganize and refine how they will love themselves and others. Their personal and professional empowerment greatly depends upon bringing qualities of forgiveness, compassion, humility, generosity, and gratitude to their evolving definition of love. This new vision can only manifest by a fervent commitment to live a self-examined life.

There are a variety of ways the personality of recovering Heroes might show up differently. We can see the notion of living more consciously manifesting cognitively, emotionally, and behaviorally. The expression of ideas happens with less urgency, replaced by a faith that more will be revealed. There is less of a tendency to lean toward some contrived certainty, with a greater capacity to hold ambiguity. There is also a greater ability to welcome diverse perspectives.

On an emotional level, recovering Heroes can have a felt sense of emotional energy in their bodies. They can also name and verbally express emotions. This opens the Hero to welcoming the emotions of others, with empathy rather than offering a solution or some form of guidance. As emotional intelligence increases, Heroes begin to suspend the dynamics of "win-lose" and "right-wrong" in their conversations. People begin to see the recovering Hero as someone with whom they can expect to be heard and understood. The Hero is likely to be perceived as a muse for deeper collaborations and co-creation.

There are several behavioral benefits characteristic of the recovering Hero. The first is a diminished use of primitive psychological defenses such as domination, excessive adaption, and distancing physically and/or emotionally. These defenses are replaced by the employment of effective boundaries. (See my book *Dare to Grow-Up* for a detailed account of effective boundaries.) Secondly, there is a diminished likelihood that authority is either abdicated or abused. Authority is held by an increased sensibility regarding whether a culture needs more encouragement and/or direction infused into it. Lastly, the recovering Hero takes joy in expressing appreciation for the commitment, efforts, and accomplishments of others.

Timothy came in to see me, feeling lost having just divorced his wife of 25 years.

"I guess I should have seen it coming. I mean Ann has not been happy for a long time. I know I spent too much time at work when the kids were little. But I thought as they went off to college, she and I could rebuild something meaningful but maybe it was too late," Timothy admitted, his tone carrying the weight of his nuptial defeat.

He became devoted to his therapy, never missing a weekly session, which proved to be one of the advantages of his heroic life. He never did anything with a cavalier attitude. He knew how to get himself totally committed regardless of the task. He detailed his childhood including a father who was a traveling salesman and seldom home. Also, he described his mother as frequently depressed, finding her in bed when returning from school. He attempted to parent his two younger siblings while not accepting anything other than academic excellence for himself. He ended up going to law school and taking a position in a prestigious law firm where he quickly became a partner.

It took some time before Timothy could feel the grief of his divorce and fractured family. These feelings were very new for him to access and talk about.

"Why do I feel like I don't really know how to be sad? I can't remember anyone helping me the way you do," he offered, his gratitude veiled by a whisper of being self-suspect.

"I want to hear how you feel about receiving my help," I added, hoping he might be willing to be a bit more transparent.

"Well, I appreciate it, but I guess I'm not sure what it says about me," he puzzled.

"I mean, shouldn't I be able to do this for myself?" he asked rhetorically, with his compulsive self-reliance showing its face.

"I want you to know that I was also a Hero in my family of origin, and the gift of defeat also visited me, and my pride almost got in the way of getting the help that I desperately needed," I shared in the hope that he might bring at least, a small measure of acceptance for his willingness to get help.

"You needed help too?" he blurted, his disbelief possessing no subtlety.

"Yes, of course. Life is too big even for heroes like us," I rejoined as we both laughed.

Timothy remained devoted to his psychological work, joining a men's group and creating several lasting friendships. He often would pause in our sessions, smile, and reiterate with a sense of confidence and disbelief that a very painful defeat, the loss of his marriage, brought him home to himself.

Belonging for the family Hero or Heroine means being willing to interrupt attempts to save, fix and deliver appropriately. Because there can be such reliance on these heroic gestures, belonging without them will make little or no sense. Initially, the Hero needs to focus on self-belonging, building up a connection to the self based on acceptance of limits and shortcomings. It will also call for learning to be kind to yourself as well as forgiving yourself and learning to ask for help, willing to show your vulnerability. These are the first steps of belonging for the Heroine. Heroes and Heroines are quite comfortable with both conditional acceptance and conditional belonging due to their confidence regarding meeting expectations. The key is to learn to be accepted by yourself unconditionally, which sets the stage for an experience of genuine belonging.

A Blessing for the Hero

You have certainly shined, again and again.
Your early offering of love was a fervent striving toward
excellence in all that you did.
You would not allow your parents to be trapped in
their suffering, constantly offering them the
distraction of your achievements.
You were the messiah.
You were condemned to conditional self-love,
with each day a new opportunity to prove your elusive worth.
You settled for being needed, one after another they came,
hoping to be supported, chosen and saved.
The role of the Hero is like wearing a special hat.
You can take it off any time you wish.
There will only be a flicker of an identity crisis.
Respond with curious eyes.
See who loves you and how their love is trying to reach you.
Pause now, be the one simply grateful for being loved.
Let it begin.

Chapter 7

Deliverance for the Lost Child

"I had become awkward and tried my best to avoid everyone. I hated attention, people asking me questions or putting me in the spotlight; I preferred to blend into the background unnoticed. I felt safer that way."

- Giovanna Fletcher -

Personal power, fulfillment, and emotional maturation greatly depend upon being able to identify and bring care to the childhood roles we occupied in our families of origin. No family is without stress; and when exasperated, the stress easily becomes a source of complex trauma for the children. Conditions such as mental illness, physical illness, addiction, and parental unavailability can lead to traumatic incidents of physical abuse, sexual abuse, and emotional abuse. Each child in the family finds his or her way into a particular role designed to express love for the parents and a mooring for safety. The more a child feels the family being out of control, the more a child will rigidly cling to one role.

I have worked with numerous folks who took on the role of Lost Child. Each time, I felt challenged, intrigued, and privileged to be invited into a healing relationship with them. **Unlike other clients whose work is to find their way back**

to their inner worlds, Lost Children are needing help to make their way out of their inner worlds. Their challenge will be to find their place in the outer world of relationships, education, and occupation.

The Lost Child mandate for loving and safety is to withdraw into their inner worlds. Their psychological imperative is to remain unobtrusive, committed to being compliant, and non-disruptive. They maintain their cloaked family profile by remaining quiet and sequestered in their rooms and other private areas where there is minimum family traffic. The Lost Children with whom I've worked have been introverted. The innate propensity for introversion is excellent compost for the construction of this family role. The child is already quite comfortable dwelling in the inner landscape. All that needs to happen is to upgrade time and energy spent in the interior world.

Let's look more closely at some of the strengths of this role:

Comfort with solitude. Lost Children know how to enjoy time alone. They easily learn how to entertain themselves, finding comfort in their own company.

Inner resources. They often develop their imaginations, intellects, and creative potentials as these endeavors don't threaten the scaffolding of the role.

Spiritual potential. In *Another Chance,* Sharon Wegscheider Cruse points out, "The quiet and isolation, the active fantasy life, the very emptiness that offers no competing relationships or satisfactions to which he has become attached – these are all circumstances that have been recognized throughout human history as conducive to spiritual growth."

Let's look more closely at some of the liabilities of this role when lived rigidly:

Excessive anonymity. Adults who took on this role in their families of origin run a risk of continuing to live from some degree of invisibility. They often don't know what it means to feel heard, understood and accepted. Loneliness easily can feel like a normal way to live.

A lost voice. Lost Children easily discover that speaking is the quickest way to violate their anonymity. As introverts, they already feel at home being frugal with the use of language. All that's needed is speaking even less, with safety and loving not being challenged. As adulthood emerges, it can be easy to become self-righteous about the alleged proper way to speak. Their verbal inhibition can take on an alleged civility. They scrutinize those indulging in free expression as holding an inordinate amount of entitlement. While working with James, a 52-year-old producing custom-built furniture, I discovered how important it can be for a Lost Child to remain voiceless. In one of our sessions, I was having difficulty hearing him and made several pleas for him to speak up. His chin dropped toward his chest and with his tone remaining singular, he said, just above a whisper, "I can't project. It will hurt my head and my eyes will feel strained." I realized that James' psyche had successfully recruited his body for some somatic assistance to secure a much-needed muted voice.

Emotional estrangement. Emotional well-being depends upon being able to feel, identify and express emotions while being heard and accepted by a trusted listener. Lost Children deem being favorably heard as either impossible or dangerous. They employ two strategies to cope with their emotions. The first is repression where the emotions are relegated to the unconscious. The second is dissociation with emotions being translated into ideas and opinions, allowing for the vulnerability of their emotions to attain some measure of protection.

Social awkwardness. When isolation is at the core of how we live, we're not quite sure what will happen when we interact with others. Being puzzled about what to say and do, accompanied by self-doubt haunts social interaction. Lost Children often become caregivers in response to confusion about giving and receiving. They decide that they can't go wrong by simply giving a lot. However, becoming a delivery system often leads to resentment and emptiness.

Impairment of genuine belonging. Nothing calls for transparency more than genuine belonging. Such relational deepening calls for clarity about feelings, emotional needs, and the expression of desire. Genuine belonging happens as Lost Children are seen, greeted, and welcomed, with their uniqueness being celebrated. The Lost Child will need to dismantle old ways of self-care and caring for others, learning viable replacements.

Potential may remain hidden. Lost Children keep so much of themselves hidden, including their gifts and talents. They easily forget they possess them. Or they create beliefs that help keep their strengths sequestered. Recently, I mentioned to a very bright young woman, still held in the role of Lost Child, that I wanted to acknowledge the sharpness of her insight and perception. She quickly responded, "Thank you, but I simply don't have the verbal skills to accurately reflect my ideas and intuitions." My heart sank as I imagined her gifts remaining cloistered, blocked from being birthed in the world.

A Reparative Path for the Lost Child

Education. I have found it very beneficial for adult Lost Children to receive information about the impact their childhood role has had upon their lives. An important reminder is how anonymity supported the need for safety and how loving was designed to prevent the Lost Child from burdening others with their needs. It is also helpful to clarify the distinction between their role and their core identity, and how influential the role can be in adulthood, issuing several significant losses.

Supporting Grief. Lost Children will need support to explore the losses, which excessive withdrawal generates regarding numerous aspects of their lives - including relationships, self-concept, personal empowerment, education, and occupation.

Learning about boundaries. It can be extremely helpful for the adult Lost Child to understand that anonymity has been employed as a primitive boundary aimed at supplying safety. I typically suggest that anonymity can be saved and used with intention, rather than an automatic form of protection. Lost Children can have control over invisibility rather than invisibility having control over them. The key is to add to their repertoire of boundaries. The first addition is simply saying "no" and "yes" authentically. The second boundary is letting go of what is out of their control. The challenge here is to access enough discernment to determine what is actually out of their control, while remaining mindful that the ego enjoys imagining that its power is limitless. As they practice saying "yes" and "no" honestly and letting go of what is out of their control, they'll find that those folks being impacted by their boundaries will likely not be pleased by the boundaries. Their boundaries may frustrate others from meeting some need or desire. Their resiliency to hold the boundary in the face of another's frustration or disapproval is another form of boundary. Boundary setting takes practice and remains a worthwhile life-long endeavor.

Building self-trust. When a defense like anonymity is employed rigidly and unconsciously, it's difficult for Lost Children to know whether they are acting in their best interest or being ruled by an attachment to invisibility. Getting clear about this distinction calls for the development of self-trust. Trust for themselves is building when they are committed to knowing their own truths. This happens as they increasingly let themselves be aware of how they feel emotionally, as well as their desires, beliefs, and values. A critical element of their truth will be their evaluation of how much anonymity they are currently employing, and how much they really need. Self-trust is also enhanced as they commit to treat themselves kindly, which happens as they increasingly interrupt disparaging judgments about how they behave. Kindness is also enacted as they eat, rest, play and work in ways that are fulfilling and sustainable.

Building trust for others. Trusting others can be more challenging for the Lost Child because it can easily lead to being more visible. A key is to remember that as a child, visibility got magically loaded with some awful stuff. The alleged nefarious outcomes included excessive vulnerability, loss of safety, and a violation of loving others. It will be important to get help unpacking the disproportionate heavy weight distributed to being visible. As that process evolves, Lost Children need to develop the capacity to be discerning regarding who to trust. Trusting others also depends upon holding the belief that the other will tell them the truth and treat them kindly. There are two caveats. The first is that they do not offer trust because someone is cute or charismatic, they must earn the trust. Secondly, they must be willing to grow a capacity to receive the acts of kindness bestowed upon them.

A safe emotional place. Lost Children need to take the delicate matter of emotional safety seriously. They have little or no experience being empathically and compassionately witnessed. Subsequently, they need to create a kind of covenant with a therapist, clergy person, coach, friend, or family member to show their emotions. It must be a place where they can trust that it's safe to make themselves visible as emotional beings.

Apprenticing to love. The Lost Child is asked to take on a task that is fitting for all of us - being an apprentice to love. Reorganizing love cognitively, emotionally, and behaviorally for the Lost Child means significantly downsizing the mandate, "I will love you by not burdening you with my presence." Before addressing how love will live when offered to lovers, self-love must be prioritized. The starting place for this love of self is simply committing to acknowledge and meet personal needs for food, rest, play, comfort, and support from others. Then, slowly focusing on how to address loving others. The initial shift sounds like: "I will do my best to be present," "I will be authentic," "I will be accountable for my behavior," "I will ask for what I need," "I will listen," and I will encourage you suspending any need to influence." Stepping into the above directions can be an immense shift for Lost Children and advance them further into the mystery of love.

A healing welcome. It is extremely beneficial for Lost Children to understand what their psychological wounding is asking for: first and foremost, not to store it in some forgotten closet in the psyche. It's just too easy for Lost Children to view their wounds as being extremely burdensome to others and serving no meaningful relational agenda. Gradually, they can learn to welcome their injury as simply an expression of their humanity and not some unfortunate aberration. When that happens, there can be a deep understanding that the power of the wound or lack of does not lie with what was inflicted. Rather, their relationship with the wound determines how mitigated its potency will be. A compassionate welcome accompanied by curiosity regarding what the wound is asking for, remains a robust source of healing. This is best accomplished by working with practitioners who offer this kind of welcome to their own wounds. Healing receives significant inspiration as Lost Children accept their wounds and are willing to learn from them. Then, while being compassionately witnessed by another they come to know what it means to be found.

Although Lost Child was not my primary role in my family of origin, I did attach to it with some tenacity. I look at my professional life, working alone for 35 years in a basement office and being very comfortable with the withdrawal. I personally know the work of learning to feel hurt without pulling in and away for a substantial amount of time. I know the pull toward the worlds of imagination and intuition, as these worlds have brought substance to my writing. However, I also know the urge driving me to sanitize reality, clinging to some purified and idyllic version. I am deeply grateful for the mentors who affirmed my dream while calling me back to the messiness of my corporeal experience. Because of their help, my dreams are less of a substitute for reality as they offer more meaning and fervor to my lived experience.

Lost Children are by definition lost to genuine belonging. The good news is that they tend to live close to themselves, engendering self-belonging. The first step is to create one good friend where you learn to receive support and interrupt your definition of love, which is not to burden others with your needs. The more Lost Children get honest about what they need and the more they learn to receive care from others, the closer they are to creating genuine belonging. It can mean accepting a life-long apprenticeship to receiving.

A Blessing for the Lost One

You have been lost in the external world.
You took up residency in the inner landscape,
resulting in compensations springing up in that inner habitat.
Fanciful visions of magic along with
chimerical spiritual assertions easily ensue.
Come back now, not abandoning your ethereal propensity,
simply allowing yourself to stand in each world,
the corporeal and the celestial.
Build a trusting relationship with at least one person.
Let that individual see you.
Learn to trust and be trusted.
Learn to give and receive, learn to hold the tension of
diverse views and to seek resolution amidst conflict.
Take your friend's hand and come to know a magic
summoning you to that place where no one goes alone.

Chapter 8

Redemption for the Scapegoat

"The Scapegoat doesn't get picked randomly or by accident. Usually, they are either sensitive, unhappy, vulnerable, ill and/or the outspoken child or whistleblower. In other words, the scapegoat is the child who refuses to look content or stay silent in the unbearable atmosphere created in the family home."

- Glynis Sherwood -

Of all the childhood roles in a family, Scapegoats are in dire need of being in repossession of their essential goodness. Scapegoats enter the family, and all too soon become aware that the Hero child has secured the position of recognition and approval. Scapegoats are rigidly attached to their role when the system is heavily stressed by addiction, illness, extreme transiency, or poverty. Unless some unfortunate situation such as an accident or illness deposes the Hero, how to belong as a recipient of parental praise eludes the Scapegoat. Any place worth pursuing seems fully occupied. It becomes apparent that something darker may be the only option.

Characteristics of Scapegoats

Negative attention. It's only too easy to view Scapegoats as incorrigible. The truth is that they simply can't imagine competing with the Hero sibling who has wrapped up everything positive. Hence, negative attention becomes preferred to no attention. There is typically no awareness that negative attention or some kind of attention is what is desired by the Scapegoat. The unconscious pursuit of negative attention can extend way beyond childhood, taking the Scapegoat hostage to a life deprived of ease and richness.

Acting-out behavior. To receive negative attention, the child begins to indulge in uncooperative and delinquent behavior. This disorderly routine can extend beyond the family to school and other social organizations, resulting in a nefarious reputation. Carrying such a stigma can negatively impact the expectations of teachers and obstruct academic success.

From role to identity. As Scapegoats indulge in unacceptable behavior, the understanding that they are anything larger than the role they occupy slowly slips away. They believe that they are bad people, reflecting the spirit of a tragic figure. Unless there is some form of therapeutic intervention, they run the risk of addiction, incarceration, and even an early death.

Outside the family. Convinced that there is no positive way to participate in the family, they rely upon peer affiliation to engender some measure of belonging. They make their way to other children who likely feel a similar frustration with family life.

Drug and alcohol abuse. Scapegoats are extremely prone to abusing street drugs and alcohol to numb the nagging feelings of rejection and hurt. They easily translate these vulnerable feelings into anger and are viewed as angry.

Connection through contention. Scapegoats don't believe that people will find them lovable, endearing, or desired. Hence, they rely on being provocative and contentious as ways to build connection to others. Unfortunately, those are not great rapport-building elements, resulting in the Scapegoat self-sabotaging their affiliation needs.

Offerings of love. Scapegoats know they cannot love their parents by what is conventionally viewed as being a success. Instead, the parents receive a negative distraction from their pain. The defiant Scapegoat can generate a myriad of disturbances and disruptions, keeping the attention of the parents away from what troubles them about themselves.

Restricted development. Scapegoats suffer both cognitive and emotional development. They take solace in deciding and proving that they are not like the Hero sibling, who may be comfortable with academic pursuits. Their intellects often do not receive the necessary guidance and encouragement that can be offered by schools and colleges. They are more interested in fine-tuning their cleverness and cunning directed at some scam or scheme to make a buck or to get someone's attention. So much of the Scapegoat's emotions remain subterranean, with only the fire of anger and rage surfacing. Repression of the more vulnerable emotions leads to unconscious emotion influencing beliefs and behaviors. It's challenging for Scapegoats to be clear about what motivates their decisions and choices and some understanding of likely outcomes. They are very prone to self-sabotage at any age, continuing to prove that their parents were correct in defining them as irredeemable. Prison populations are typically stockpiled with Scapegoats, continuing to live out their unconscious self-sabotage.

Restorative Measures for the Scapegoat

Psychological education. Scapegoats benefit immensely when learning that they have been playing a role. They will need solid therapeutic support as they gradually release a way to see themselves that has likely been confirmed by parents, relatives, and a host of authority figures. They can gradually accept that feelings of self-deprecation were part of the role and not a reflection of who they are. It can be very helpful for them to view the entire system, especially the place occupied by the Hero sibling.

Getting acquainted with vulnerability. Scapegoats typically show a tough guy, tough gal persona. In a trusting therapeutic relationship, they might dare to let go of a much-cherished bravado. Allowing themselves to get close to hurt feelings will make them feel more vulnerable. Claiming their authentic selves will be frightening as well as being supported for doing so. The core of identity includes not being seen, scoffed, and labeled incorrigible. There will be the vulnerability of a lost hope to be accepted and appreciated. If their parents defined them as hardened and hopeless, they then need to feel the vulnerability of betraying their parents as they reclaim their essential worth.

Moving out of delusion. Scapegoats typically build a case in support of their non-conventional and iconoclastic lifestyle. The delusion is that they have not betrayed themselves as so many others have done. They create an ethos condemning those who sold out to the system, acquiring a formal education and a house with a white picket fence. They glorify their errant ways as testimony to their courage and honesty. What they need to get honest about is how self-sabotaging they have lived, dictated by their family role. Beneath all the rhetoric is the claim that their Hero sibling wasn't all those folks made them out to be – claiming Heroes are nice guys selling out.

Welcoming a measure of self-love. Of all the childhood roles, the Scapegoat has the greatest challenge engendering self-love. The Scapegoat's ego has settled into being especially bad, avoiding any semblance of being pedestrian or plain vanilla. They are also convinced that there is no constructive way to receive attention. Scapegoats need to return to the main purpose of the role again and again, an offering of a loving negative distraction. As such, their damaging self-concept was only a story attached to the role. They can begin to be mindful of self-deprecating narratives and learn to interrupt them as bad stories, saying nothing about reality. Such interruptions are the compost for growing love for the self.

Building genuine support. Scapegoats possess natural rapport building skills, especially with peers. They can learn how to deepen their capacity for empathy and carry their sensitivity as a strength. They can be great allies for those feeling disenfranchised, defeated and alone. They can learn that they are deserving of the same support they offer others.

Death of a sacrificial lamb. Scapegoats are the sacrificial lamb of the family. They are willing to sacrifice themselves for the good of the family. Healing comes to their souls as they accept that their sacrifice is no longer needed and learn the distinction between necessary and unnecessary sacrifice. Integrating this understanding of sacrifice can easily morph into a practice of care for the body, mind, and spirit.

The emergence of inner authority. Scapegoats live in the illusion that they have escaped the dictates and expectations of authority figures. The truth is that their compulsive insurrections have negatively tied them to external authority. As they allow the need for defiance to subside, they can begin to develop inner authority. The seeds of which are germinated by asking: What do I love? What is my love asking for? What are my gifts and strengths? How might my gifts serve? To what or whom am I willing to give myself? What feeds my soul?

When the dark path is reinforced by peers, Scapegoats can struggle to find their way back to the light of their essential goodness. It behooves educators, clergy, counselors, and coaches to be alert to a client's description of their family of origin. The moment I hear a sibling defined as a sure winner, I become vigilantly curious about the possibility of being in the presence of a Scapegoat. Human potential practitioners are the most valuable resource for Scapegoats. It's just too difficult for Scapegoats to wrap their heads around what happened to them in their families of origin. However, anyone who understands the various ways children love can offer a Scapegoat an invitation to step out of this debilitating role.

Justin, a 19-year-old college student, came in to see me wearing his hair shoulder length looking like it had been forgotten for some time. He had on jean jacket and black denim trousers hanging low enough to reveal most of the crease of his buttocks. He dropped into the chair in my office with a resonant thud, suggesting this may be all you will be hearing of me. He made an entrance not concealing his aversion to be in my company.

Although I had no idea where the session might go, I had grown a resiliency for being in the presence of tough guy energy, knowing there was tons of humanity just below the surface. I was willing to let go, knowing how little control I had to call for the courage it would take for Justin to drop into his core. All the time I was wondering if I might be in the presence of someone hip deep into the role of a Scapegoat.

"So, Justin, tell me why you're here, what brings you to

me?" I asked, fairly certain I was about to hear how someone coerced him into this session.

"Well, you know it's not my fucken idea," he quipped, a side of his lip tucked up, eyes darting around the room and likely hoping his language would disarm me.

"Yeah, I hear you. It's not my fucken idea either," I retorted, thankful for the neighborhood I grew-up in, which in times like this seemed more valuable than my academic training.

"Do you talk to all your clients like that?" Justin blurted, attempting to control the conversation.

"No, no I only talk to clients who fucken talk like that." I teased, wondering if he might be willing to relax his untethered bravado.

"Wow, and you call yourself a shrink!" he returned, letting me know he wasn't quite sure what to do with me, which I believed could be helpful to the both of us.

"Yeah, some say I'm a shrink. What do you call yourself?" I rejoined, hoping for some small measure of honesty.

"Shit, I don't know. My mom pleaded with me to come here. I'm doing it for her. I've got a lot of other things I'd rather be doing, believe me," Justin asserted, letting me know he was feeling a bit lost and willing to honor his mother's request.

"Why would your mother want you to come hang out with me?" I asked, wondering if he could continue to be honest.

"I got suspended for a semester. My grades aren't great and I kicked this guy's ass in my dorm for saying shit about my girl. I think my mom's worried about a lot, not just me. My father lost his job and he's drinking a lot," he explained, his shoulders dropping, offering a few seconds of eye contact.

"Sounds to me like your mother might be experiencing some real stress in her life right now," I offered, hoping he would hear my empathy for his mother.

"Oh yeah, I guess my older brother is the only bright light for her. He's about to graduate from an ivy league college and he was captain of the lacrosse team. Sean has really made her happy, well, as happy as she can be," he offered, his sadness regarding his mother's situation being palpable.

Justin went on talking about his family, pausing regularly to validate all that his mother gives to the family. When I told him the session was about to end and asked if he wanted to come back, he responded in true Scapegoat fashion, "Yeah, I think I will. There wasn't much psychological bullshit that went on."

I was somewhat surprised as Justin returned regularly for his weekly sessions. Once we went over the role of the Scapegoat, he quickly saw how much he decided that anything positive was going Sean's way. He was able to understand that there is not a limited amount of love in a family and that there was surely enough for him. He gradually let go of his strong anti-authority posturing. He learned to employ a Scapegoat's natural inclination to discriminate authenticity from someone leaning into the script of a role. Both of which strengthened his capacity to trust in a discerning fashion.

He gradually allowed the call to be a sacrificial lamb die off. In its place, he learned about the difference between necessary and unnecessary sacrifice. Most of all, he opened to his essential goodness, allowing for redemption due to him.

Of the 4 family roles, the Scapegoat likely has the most natural inclination to create genuine belonging since they easily generate rapport with peers. The challenge will be to step away from acting out with an anti-authority attitude in order to create bonding with others. Another vital ingredient will be moving out of attachment to receiving negative attention to truly believing that they are worthy of honest, positive regard. It can be helpful to be clear that you initially stepped into this role for two reasons - the role of Hero was likely occupied and you decided to love by offering a negative distraction for your parent's pain. In order to genuinely belong you will need to construct a new way of loving. One example might be to utilize your natural propensity to create coalitions, allowing yourself to become a supportive resource for those with whom you desire to belong.

A Blessing for Soul Retrieval

You gave your soul away out of love.
Now, it is time to reclaim it out of love.
This idea that there was something wrong with you was never true.
You acted out, attempting to confirm the insinuation that
you belonged on the path of the sacrificial lamb.
Begin the retrieval process by living your ability
to craft genuine friendship.
Allow your antipathy for authority to subside as it was simply
circumscribed by the role you played.
Now, find a measure of inner authority.
From this interior sovereignty, your values and your heart's desire
find what hungers to be born.
You will find your soul in whatever you create.

Chapter 9

Maturation for the Mascot

"Some of us look grown-up but aren't. We walk around with suits and briefcases and car keys and annuities. But inside, we are five. Ten. Twelve. Sixteen. We sit in boardrooms, travel the world, even write books. But we are kids, still playing dress-up, playing house. Our bodies matured but our minds did not."

- S. Rufus -

The youngest child in a family often occupies the role of Mascot. If the stress in the family is not excessively severe, the child in this role knows how to play, have fun, and bring lightness to family life. This child's gift of love is an offering of endless comedy with the price being arrested development. However, if family stress builds, the Mascot hides fear and confusion behind a permanently painted smile. Family members get to release pent-up tension as they laugh and hoot at the antics of the family jokester. In fact, the jocularity stimulated by the Mascot may be the only authentic emotions expressed in the family.

Sharon Wegscheider-Cruse suggests, "You don't have to be with a family more than a few minutes to know which child is playing this part. He may act cute and helpless, or interrupt and do 'crazy' things. He may beguile you or bedevil you, but he's very hard to ignore." If the Mascot locks into his or her role without repair, then the repertoire of slapstick trails them into adulthood. Such a primitive way to cope will have varied injurious implications.

Challenges Facing the Mascot

Faces significant levels of denial. As Mascots view their role as the essence of their identity, it becomes very easy to deny that there is any kind of a problem. Their role exempted them from living life on life's terms, having to face the tension and ambiguity of real-life situations. Why give up simply having a good time?

Often misdiagnosed. Mascots often go misdiagnosed initially with ADHD and later with manic episodes.

Learning impediment. Remaining a clown striving to engage and distract classmates with a variety of antics will not lend itself to classroom learning. If Mascots are lucky, they might see a formal education offering a ticket to professional advancement but likely lack the depth to see their education as possibly opening a door to a vocation.

Risks being locked into the *puer/puella* personality. The *puer/puella* or eternal boy/girl can become a life-long persona. Mascots have repressed their ability for introspection so as not to allow anything that might interrupt their parade.

Loses friends. As their friends grow and mature, Mascots remain gridlocked in an infantile pattern. Friends who have moved on from juvenile mannerisms and responses no longer find the Mascot all that entertaining.

Loss of intimacy. As Mascots experience a measure of arrested development, their capacity for in-depth relationships can be severely restricted. They likely will lack an ability to offer genuine empathy, address conflict and know how to offer an understanding of themselves to the relationship.

Immature spirituality. Convinced that there are no real complex questions, Mascots either ignore their spiritual lives or reduce it to periodic church attendance accompanied by a perfunctory adherence to dogma.

Healing for the Mascot

Psychological education. Mascots can gain a great deal by understanding their role in a stressed system. Of course, such understanding will not come easily since it is the antithesis of the Mascot's way to cope. The hope is that they can value their propensity for lightness without the illusion that lightness can address all that life has to offer. An essential learning is that they were over-protected as children and offered a deluded sense of reassurance that all was well.

Grieving. The more Mascots learn about their role and the status in their family of origin, they begin to identify losses. Their losses include honest disclosure about family challenges, encouragement to access inner strengths and resources, and the modeling of effective coping mechanisms. Although losses are not easy to address, it very well might mean the beginning of Mascots' daring to get honest about what dwells within.

Acceptance of intuition. As Mascots work their recovery, they may access memories of vague intuitions they experienced as a child. These old intuitions likely were informing the child about the stress facing the family. They can begin to trust the pulse of their current intuitions.

Scared and confused. As their compulsion for humor subsides, the emotions of fear and confusion likely surface. They can learn to shamelessly feel these feelings. A key is to understand that as a child they did not possess enough inner resource to navigate these feelings. Confusion likely resulted because their intuitions conflicted with the parental reassurance they were receiving. Fear would also get ignited due to the incongruence of their experience.

Practicing silence with breath. A helpful intrapersonal practice is to simply explore being silent and breathing when interacting with others. A first step is to relinquish jocularity and learn to hold the ensuing tension by focusing on the breath. It will be a sizable leap for Mascots to let go of comic engagement and focus on their interior world in the presence of others.

Releasing tension. Mascots are very familiar with working with tension by slipping into a comedy routine. New methods for releasing tension will be critical in the support of emotional maturity. Deep breathing, exercise, yoga, tracking internal sensations, meditation, therapeutic massage, and acupuncture are helpful ways to address the release of tension.

Easing into ambiguity. The comic relief exercised by Mascots derails them from learning how to relate to the ambiguous nature of what gives meaning and depth to life. Hence, benchmarks for maturation - such as wrestling with an ability to be authentic, courageous, and compassionate - are not entertained by Mascots or are endeavors receiving minimal attention. Mascots can gradually learn to entertain what both gives meaning and is ambiguous by eliminating hilarity and moving gradually toward holding more curiosity. Ultimately, their relationship with ambiguity can unfold a mature spirituality - one galvanized by curiosity, devotion, personal values, and a longing for unity consciousness.

Unlike the other family roles, Mascots are encouraged not to grow up. The other roles certainly carry some impediment to maturation, but no one is viewing those roles as appropriately infantile. At least one parent is benefiting or distracted from the Mascot's shenanigans as well as attempting to protect the Mascot from the turmoil in the family. If Mascots experience enough loss or pain, they may seek the help and support that can point them in the direction of their own maturation.

This was the case with Stephen, a 50–year–old manager of a retail chain, married for 20 years with 3 children. He entered my office with a large grin on his face and moved toward a seat with a swagger suggesting he was extremely comfortable.

"So, Stephen, tell me a bit about what brings you here. I must say, most people don't come here looking quite as cheery as you do," I remarked, wondering how genuine that grin was.

"Well, I'm always pretty cheerful. I mean who benefits if we get all down and dreary?" he suggested, with his grin stretching further than I thought his face could accommodate.

"Okay, cheery or not, tell me more about what brings you here," I invited, becoming mascot–alert.

"I don't think my marriage is in any real trouble, but my wife thinks there's something I should look at. Specifically, how I respond to people," Stephen described, not relinquishing his grip on that grin.

"Does your wife not appreciate how you respond to her or people in general?" I inquired, wondering how much he had understood his wife's feedback.

"Oh no, she's talking about how I respond to our children as well as to her," he explained, his grin losing some of its extension and luster.

"Can you say more about these responses and why they obviously annoy your wife?" I encouraged, noticing the tapping of his foot becoming more rapid.

"She says I'm never serious, that I make jokes or react lightly when family members are expressing something serious. I mean the folks at work think I'm an easy-going guy," he claimed, seeming to hope that his work persona would get my attention.

I went on to ask questions about his family of origin and his siblings. He spoke about a high-achieving older brother and an older sister who was prone to acting-out in some way. He concluded by describing himself as the youngest; and with palpable pride and enthusiasm, he recounted how his parents insisted that he perform as song and dance for family and guests at holidays. He stressed how much he saw their request for the show as a loving act on behalf of his parents. It was feeling more and more apparent I was hearing a Mascot offer an account of his childhood.

Before introducing him to the role of the Mascot, we explored what responses people need when they feel challenged or distraught. I affirmed how much he was attempting to care and support people by introducing levity into the conversation about their concerns.

"I don't get what I would do. I mean I don't want to awfulize the situation or make it worse," Stephen puzzled, leaning forward with what appeared to be curiosity regarding the alternatives.

"I'm with you. This is not about awfulizing or bringing more drama to the situation. It's mostly about empathy, feeling into the struggle of the speaker. And simply acknowledging what you hear the person addressing," I offered, wondering how ready he was to interrupt a compulsive use of jocularity.

"I guess I tell myself that if I'm really caring I should have a solution for them and I don't. It makes me feel badly," he admitted, the grin disappearing, with more of an opening happening.

"What a great thing to say to someone you love, 'I really want to give you a solution to your problem and I don't have one,'" I suggested.

"Is that enough?" he worried, curious if it would be a sufficient offering.

"It's the truth; and if it's offered with compassion, it's a valued offering. You can listen with your heart, letting the speaker know you are with them as you acknowledge their struggle and allow them to come forward with their feelings. However, let's have you practicing with yourself. You have a great smile. Slowly, allow that smile to express what is true for you in your heart. If you feel glad, thankful, or celebratory, let your smile deliver the truth of those feelings. Let the smile gently release when you feel sad, scared, or angry. Your family will likely feel more comfortable as you allow your external expression to tell the story of what is happening inside you," I explained. Concerned that I might be offering too much new material, I allowed for the silence that ensued.

"Wow, I feel like I've been living half of a life. I'm bright enough to figure out that life is more than smiles and happy times. What have I been doing?" Stephen asked, with a note of self-admonishment.

"You've been loving the best you know how. None of us get love just right. Love is always calling us to understand it in some new way, it remains just out of reach," I suggested, hoping he could gently hold what he was discovering.

I went on to tell him that I saw his large heart and we were mostly talking about learning how to carry such a heart so that those whom he loved could truly be fully touched by it. He worked only a short time with me. After some months passed, I received an email: "I'm keeping that grin where it belongs."

The Mascot runs the risk of living a life of superficial belonging dictated by fun and humor. Self-belonging becomes critical for Mascots if they can drop beneath the jocularity and make peace with their fear and vulnerability. From those depths, they can at least begin to navigate a sense of belonging with themselves. Their superficial connection to themselves must be replaced by personal values, beliefs, and desires. They will also need to reorganize how they love. They need to replace offering others the distraction of humor and jocularity with learning how to be authentically present, being able to be with their own deep emotions as well as that of others.

A Blessing for Rightsizing

We are all either oversizing or undersizing.
We do it for love.
You likely promised to remain someone's baby.
Your job is not to remain someone's baby.
From the undersized vantage point, life feels too big.
Life is too big for all of us.
Your role exempted you from living life on life's terms.
You reduced life to a series of opportunities to play and have fun.
There is an adult in you waiting to take his or her rightful place.
You will need to get honest about how you feel, what attracts your curiosity and what you are willing to learn.
Your rightsizing depends upon an honest inventory of your strengths and limits.
Allow this apprenticeship of rightsizing to bring you closer to yourself and to others.

Chapter 10

Parentification

"I was forced to grow up too soon. This is for any of you out there who are victims of 'parentification.' Those of you who had to 'be the parent' instead of having a parent. The ones who had to take on more responsibility than you should ever have to at such a young age. Whose childhood was unfairly stolen from them."

- Jessica Evans -

Parentification of children happens when parents are either unwilling and/or unable to effectively parent their children. Parental absence may occur because of mental illness, addiction, arrested development, medical issues, or unavailability due to work or travel. Parentified Children step into the parental void. The attempt to take on parental responsibilities snatches children out of childhood, disengaging from a normal developmental process.

Let's look at 3 expressions of Parentification:

Not Enough Parenting

This form of Parentification is due to parental neglect. The children take on the responsibility of parenting themselves. In lieu of parental guidelines and expectations, children rely upon their own understanding of self-care and social acuity. Children may be challenged to eat properly, rest, attend to personal hygiene and perform academically. Often, parentified kids will take their cues from peers who are being parented effectively.

Parentified Children who are neglected are not receiving valuable information about boundaries. They won't be clear about when a boundary serves their unique preferences and needs, or what kind of boundary is appropriate regarding providing safety. Not being the recipient of nurturance will leave them puzzled about the renewing power of nurturance and what it means to have needs and receive support from others. There will also be uncertainty about the power of receiving encouragement, knowing that someone holds the faith in whom they are. Lastly, they can be baffled about providing adequate limits that delay immediate gratification in the name of securing some valued future outcome.

There can be a level of severe confusion about the price paid for being neglected. The confusion is amplified if children ignore the fact that they are neglected and focus on the freedom afforded them by their parents' lack of responsibility. The most prevalent coping mechanism aimed at dealing with these loses is increased levels of pretending. They run a high risk of pretending they need no one and that they know exactly what they're doing.

Sometimes, Parentified Children will create romantic liaisons with their teenage peers. These adolescent connections are attempts to anesthetize feelings of abandonment and inadequacy. The child waffles between indulging in a compulsive self-reliance and extreme dependency in an effort to feel loved and wanted. In either case, children are attempting to prove they know how to have real relationships or demonstrate that they need no one. Both cause them to suffer from a deep level of pretending.

Unless Parentified Children who suffered from neglect

seek out therapeutic help, early coping mechanisms get amplified in later years. The one area where feelings of inadequacy push to the surface and pretending begins to run thin is in relationships. In the absence of early parental involvement, Parentified Children have limited self-care skills and an underdeveloped aptitude for rapport building. Several strategies are often employed to cope with feeling relationally deficient. One such strategy is simply deciding that relationships are basically frivolous and a waste of time. "Why get into fraternizing when there is so much to get accomplished."

The second strategy, which rolls easily off the first one, is to develop a strong task orientation toward life. The vulnerability of not knowing what to do in relationships is replaced by protocols, formulas and plans for getting stuff done.

The third strategy is to ramp up a need for control, which is an attempt at keeping old feelings of helplessness at bay. This controlling energy can drive a compulsive striving to get things right. This striving energy is meant to numb the ever-present feeling of not being enough.

Functional Parentification

Let's look at a second level of parentification which carries more responsibilities often delegated to Parentified Children as the result of not enough parenting. Besides taking care of themselves, they can be asked or required to attend to fundamental domestic tasks such as cooking, cleaning, shopping for groceries and even paying bills. This level of parentification may also include the care of younger siblings. Parentified Children take on the responsibility of helping with homework, assisting in getting ready for school, and preparing meals. This dimension of parentification asks children to not only pretend that they can take care of themselves but also to pretend they know how to take care of other children.

Too Much Parent and Not Enough

Some children don't get enough parenting or are neglected by parents; while other children may get too much parent, which translates into abuse. The parents' emotional needs take precedent over those of the child. When this happens, children receive a greater call out of childhood. Now, they not only need to take care of themselves but also care for their parents. They are strapped with confusion about how to take care of themselves as well as how to care for the adult. The child moves into the role of friend, confidant, surrogate parent, or surrogate spouse. This form of parentification is often referred to as emotional incest and is typically accompanied by deep feelings of inadequacy, which can haunt well into adulthood. There is a higher likelihood of emotional incest is single-parent homes.

Parentified Children often suffer from a gnawing, amorphous sense of low self-esteem, never quite feeling they are enough. As adults, they may avoid relationships either because they are convinced that they are unlovable or because they believe the past will be reproduced where they are consumed by the other person. The latter fear is the result of the child's emotional boundaries having been violated. They may see a relationship happening only if they are able to give enough.

Victims of emotional incest either avoid relationships or become caregivers. Caregiving affords them the opportunity to be in a relationship without fully participating. They reproduce the early neglect of their emotional needs by only focusing on the other person. If partners and spouses continue to inform them about their needs, they can continue to deliver and avoid the inherent ambiguity of real intimacy along with the typical conflict of diverse needs.

Abused Parentified Children come from a void of genuine adult responsibility. These children learned early how to become overly responsible as they attempted to off- balance the under-responsibility of the parent. Hence, they are prone to believing they are responsible for the happiness of others. They can easily chastise themselves for the troubled feelings of friends and family. This over responsible inclination is accompanied by weak or excessively permeable boundaries, leaving them confused about where they begin and where they end.

Both neglected and abused Parentified Children often carry a feeling of being fraudulent into adulthood. When a childhood pattern of pretending is assimilated into the psyche, in can be difficult to discern what one is truly capable of.

The Healing of Parentification

The real story. Parentified Children need help as adults to examine the actual story of their childhoods. They need support to clarify the level of neglect and/or abuse that took place. There is likely going to be a level of denial of how much their parents abdicated their responsibility to actually parent. Moving through such denial needs to be a gradual process, gently honoring the distorted view held by the adult who was parentified.

Rightsizing self-concept. This inventory should include downsizing the idealization of self-reliance, exploring its benefits as well as its capacity to generate emotional isolation. A review of how much they were asked to operate out of their competency level is an important way to further an honest account. Such an account should include forgiving themselves for pretending as a way to cope with a very challenging situation.

Grief. There will be a need to find permission to feel the losses of an unlived childhood, losses such as parental guidance and significant attachment and the loss of time for play. There is also the loss of trusting that they could embark upon adventures with peers and return to the security of a home held together by a real parent. Also, they lost the freedom that comes with the trust that someone more knowledgeable and mature is primarily responsible to provide them with care.

Somatic work. They very well may need some somatic work to regulate the nervous system as they continue to come into the reality of their pasts. It can also be helpful to relieve the need to detach from the here and now by engaging in dissociation. This kind of work will generate more resiliency to over-come feeling out of control as they access varied emotions. The vulnerability regarding feeling emotions is due to the understanding that they would likely be left alone when accessing deep feelings.

Develop an inner parent. As adults, Parentified Children run the risk of reproducing the past by neglecting themselves. The neglect may show up regarding dental care, regular medical checkups, excessive work habits, confusion about personal limits and not knowing how to ask for help. This inner parent knows who to ask for help and allows for good boundaries by saying "no" and "yes" authentically. This inner parent identifies and provides activities that are nurturing, such as a walk in the woods, a sauna experience, therapeutic massage, a nap and simply calling a friend. It is extremely healing to take on the responsibility of being self-encouraging, interrupting self-ridicule and self-blame.

Develop a reliable support system. This is a critical element in the healing of parentification. They learned early that there are no reliable support systems. Hence, they face the fact that someone or some group offers more than their parents, which from a child's perspective, is a betrayal of the parent. The therapeutic agenda will be to find the courage to prioritize self-loyalty in place of parental loyalty. They will need to develop a discerning trust for others, which translates into identifying who will tell them the truth and treat them kindly.

Learn to fully participate in a relationship. Full participation calls for interrupting compulsive caretaking and replacing it with one's own desire and learning to negotiate and compromise from that desire. It also means learning to identify and employ effective boundaries, the starting point being willing to say "no" and "yes" authentically. These learnings will entail feeling vulnerable as the template provided by caretaking falls away, calling for resiliency to bear the unfavorable responses of those receiving your boundaries.

Cope with the ensuing ambiguity. Due to the lack of parental guidance, parentification can lead to a kind of literalism of life's deepest mysteries. Overly concrete answers and solutions are formulated to address ephemeral issues such as freedom, loyalty, spirituality, and love. There can be a tendency toward self-righteousness to cope with the shame of not knowing. Parentified children will be served by growing a resilient holding regarding uncertainty as well as sustaining curiosity rather than remaining smug in the face of ambiguity.

Quite often, adult Parentified Children have carved some niche where they feel confident and secure. It may be a professional arena or a hobby. They know that in a safe place they don't have to worry about being confused, pretending to know or needing help. However, their relational lives, which cannot be reduced to a simple set of regulations, will likely be where they face the greatest opportunity to welcome some healing. It will mean finding the courage to call off their moratorium on noticing they need help and acquiring it. Lastly, upon being self-examining, adults who were parentified as children need to see themselves on a continuum, reflecting a degree of parentification.

Parentification is all very familiar to me. I was a Parentified Child. My early understanding of it happened during a medical visit for my father who was being treated for poor circulation. I was sixteen at the time. When the physician came out to speak to my mother about my father's condition, she stepped back several paces leaving me in the path of receiving the doctor's message. It would be some years before I would become more curious about where I came from. Although my adolescence was reflective of athletic and academic success, the striving instilled in me by both the roles of Hero and Parentified Child left me feeling an unquenchable inadequacy.

It wasn't until I was 29 did I succumb to a deep need to get help. It was likely that the death of one daughter and the birth of another completely disabled that brought me to an undeniable sense of defeat. Since I had been groomed to pretend that I knew what I was doing, I was engulfed in shame as there was simply no more room for pretense. I learned that my mother likely felt quite frightened about being a parent, fearing some level of failure as well as bearing the scars of paternal neglect. The stage was set for calling an oldest son into the role of attempting to parent his mother. A task doomed to failure.

I recall my therapist asking me to bring some pictures of childhood to our next session. I showed her a picture of me when I was 12. She said she saw a 12-year-old boy who looked 17. When I showed her a picture of me at seventeen, she responded, "He looks like a contemporary of yours at 29."

I was immediately curious about how did I come to look older than I was. I will always remember her words.

"The psyche holds a powerful energy. When you were convinced that you should be older than you were, your psyche likely enrolled your body to help play the role of being older. You emotionally responded to the family's need for you to exit childhood, so you did, in mind and body. Now it's time to return. It's not too late for you to reclaim the childhood that was always yours," explained Joyce, her compassion and encouragement being palpable as she leaned forward, clearly convinced that the task of reclaiming my childhood was certainly attainable.

"How do I begin?" I puzzled, with the photographs swirling in my brain.

"You've already begun. You're here seeking help, admitting that there might be someone larger than you who can assist and guide you," Joyce explained, her words landing on me as a trustworthy reassurance.

I'm not sure if I'll ever completely reclaim my lost childhood. However, I did get incremental help along the way. I recall my old professor Ken Blanchard saying, "I never make major decisions alone," which went a long way to interrupt my compulsive self-reliance. I feel considerably less urgent when facing the unknown. I stay as close as possible to the mantra, "More will be revealed"; and typically it is. However, I can't help but wonder what I'll look like as I age.

A Blessing for Coming Home

As a parentified child, I was homeless.
My mandate was to bring shelter to a parent or a sibling,
while occasionally stepping into the delusion I could parent myself.
As I provided for others, I became increasingly distant from
my need to be remembered and held.
I took up residency in the voice, "I am he who provides,"
"I am he who delivers."
The seduction came by way of a consideration that anyone
who offered so much must be so much, and certainly not homeless.
It took a bit to feel the emptiness of being the one who delivers
and feel how far I lived from my own body.
Maybe, it was the growing resentment that got my attention.
How much could I tolerate being forgotten?
And then came the epiphany that was waiting for me.
I am the one who forgot me. I had ascribed so much value
to being the delivery that I forgot about my own soul.
It was time to come home, come home to my longing,
and allow myself to be touched and moved by all that life
offered me.

Chapter 11

The Glorified Paternal

"The psychological absence of fathers can be nearly as devastating as physical absence. When fathers are alive but not a predictable presence actively participating in their daughter's lives the relationship becomes a permanent 'maybe.'"

- Victoria Secunda -

What about fathers and daughters? We seem more able to get our teeth into other family dynamics. Stories of fathers and sons, mothers and sons, and mothers and daughters all seem to reveal themselves more vividly. I have worked with many fathers of daughters and many daughters in my counseling practice over the years. Having raised two daughters myself, I am especially interested in the topic of fathering daughters.

Let's look more closely at the ways fathers have explained their parenting of daughters. Most of the fathers I worked with were residing in the home with their partners and daughters.

Here are some responses I received when questioning men about their relationship with their daughters. "Well, since my wife is female, I just think she knows more about parenting our daughter." This was a very common response; and when it received further examination, it became obvious that these dads were afraid of feeling inadequate or even failing. When the fathers got honest, they admitted that deference to the mother was a lot about hoping to feel less burdened by parental responsibilities.

Another popular reaction was, "I work a lot and do my best making sure everyone in the family gets their needs met. I don't get to spend much time with the girls." Here, the dads find comfort locking into the role of provider, doing what is most comfortable. The sanctuary of the role probably mitigates the likelihood of failing at fathering daughters. Again, like the first explanation, parental responsibilities are toned down.

Here is a third response, not quite as common as the other two. "I don't really know what to say. I mean, I never really had female friends nor sisters. I just had a series of girlfriends," they explain, often accompanied by a forced chuckle. Our initial consideration of this explanation focuses on the lack of female relationships. However, when we deepen the inquiry, it becomes obvious that the fathers are concerned about somehow sexualizing their daughters since sex has been a major way of relating to the opposite gender.

It became important to address this fear of sexualizing daughters. The dads I worked with were not aware of how natural it is for fathers to feel sexually attracted to their maturing daughters. Once they got over the shock of this realization, we discussed their responsibility regarding their attraction.

Foremost, I encourage fathers to hold their attraction shamelessly. If they shame themselves, they begin to physically and/or emotionally distance, which does not help daughters feel good about themselves.

Secondly, I remind them that they might be projecting shame onto the daughter, then sending non-verbal glances and facial gestures as well as shaming utterances to the daughter. A female client recalled descending the stairs on her way to the high school prom, at which point she asked her father how she looked, hoping to receive a compliment. Her father responded, "You look like a slut." Another female client remembered her father saying, "Don't ever sit on my lap again."

My third recommendation is to employ the kind of boundary that allows for the expression of warmth and care and prohibits covert or overt sexual advances. Covert conveyances include lude glances and facial gestures. Overt sexual approaches suggest some form of erotic contact including passionate kissing, petting and genital contact. Boundaries that allow for affection and prevent sexual contact are especially important as daughters approach puberty, as they explore their relationship to the opposite gender. It's natural that daughters become somewhat seductive during this period and critical that fathers do not read the seduction as a call to be sexual.

We have identified at least three ways that fathers emotionally distance from their daughters. Fathers fear feeling inadequate or failing at fathering daughters. They don't want to feel burdened by parental responsibility, and they fear sexualizing their daughters.

Deciding that there is something wrong with themselves and aggrandizing fathers is the most natural way daughters cope with emotionally absent fathers. They maintain paternal loyalty while betraying themselves. By diminishing themselves and projecting favorable qualities to the father, daughters are doing what makes them feel most safe when facing paternal absence. When daughters decide they are not enough to account for the inaccessibility of the father, they create two beliefs that allegedly make them feel safe. First, they maintain their loyalty to the father which in a magical way suggests they are being good daughters who do not deserve being abandoned. Secondly, if the father's absence is allegedly due to the daughter being undeserving, then she supposedly maintains some control over the relationship with her father, since she could possibly improve.

A projection is a process of displacing or attributing one's own feelings and beliefs to another person. These feelings and beliefs can be positive or negative. If the original glorified projection onto the father is not addressed, girls become women who project paternal glorification to lovers, teachers, coaches, bosses, mentors, and gurus. They can continue to account for any success or competency they possess as a reflection of the good graces of some benevolent male. This pattern of a woman's self-degradation accompanied by the aggrandizement of some male can persist throughout life. Interrupting it typically calls for therapeutic support.

The therapeutic process is aimed at reclaiming and restoring the girl's sense of lovability and competency while creating a non-idyllic profile of the father's humanity. As the father's glorification peals away, a woman might feel she is betraying her father. A critical reminder is that she is merely betraying the inflated version of her father. She is simply claiming personal power due to her willingness to honor both her father's strengths and shortcomings.

In some cases, a woman's mother was either abusive or neglectful for a variety of reasons. This often results in the father being perceived as the only possible candidate for performing as a caring and supportive parent, which can lead to an elevation of the father's character. Under the circumstances, the father's importance allegedly mitigates the loss of a trusted maternal figure. The girl runs the same risk of projecting to any male who appears to be reassuring and concerned. The magic attributed to the absent father is easily projected to another male. When this happens, life is viewed as more manageable due to his guidance. The world might even be seen as safer. The energy driving the original projection continues in the hope of delivering the same favorable outcomes.

To strengthen her capacity to save herself rather than rely upon the benevolence and prowess of a mentor or teacher, she will need to learn to deconstruct hierarchy. Any projection of paternal aggrandizement will entail a hierarchal profile, postering the male somewhere above. I recommend an honest inquiry regarding her attachment to hierarchy, guided by several poignant questions: How has my attachment to hierarchy served me? What do I fear about stepping out of hierarchy? What can I employ for support rather than a hierarchal structure? Do the boundaries implicit in hierarchy protect me from real intimacy?

It might also be helpful to understand the distinction between hierarchal support and peer support. The former locates the power of giving support to one person. The latter distributes power to the self, and trusted friends and colleagues. This more egalitarian approach will likely be more informal and mutually supportive, making it more intimate.

What About the Recipients of Glorified Paternal Projections?

The recipients of a glorified paternal projection may not be doing anyone any favors, including themselves. Most obvious, they are colluding with the disempowerment of the protege. This runs contrary to anyone up to the business of genuine eldering. More subtle and possibly more seductive is the impact of owning and living with the projection. Taking on such a projection can put a man in an adversarial relationship with his own humanity. In the presence of adoring eyes, it can become very easy to deny personal limits and shortcomings, which can place self-care in jeopardy. As a recipient of the protege's homage, the teacher is ready to have an enthusiastic relationship with answers allegedly adding to his mastery. When this occurs, curiosity easily loses its allure, with the mentor slipping into the comfort of contrived certainty.

When an inquiry sacrifices important questions, a relationship with the archetype of the Fool has likely been forfeited. It is the Fool who knows how to live in a robust relationship with the unknown and in ambiguity. An inquiry becomes more collaborative when induced with questions. Only the Fool has an uncensored connection with the unknown, the first step on the path to wisdom. I'm comforted by a teacher telling fool stories depicting his own buffoonery.

As the protege's dependency is encouraged, the mentor's need for the student's admiration builds with several unfortunate consequences. The first is a more tenacious need to control the protege, so she doesn't take her glorified projection elsewhere. Secondly, the mentor is now more invested in the protege's devotion to him rather than what it truly means to serve the protege. This exterior referencing of his worth runs the risk of undermining the mentor's power to hold his own essential worth.

Fathers

I don't want to end this work without acknowledging the fathers' befuddlement by what it means to authentically show up for their daughters. We, fathers need to be aware of what we can offer to our daughters. Our emotional involvement in the lives of our daughters reminds them that they are worth it. That is a huge message! It impacts how daughters see themselves, including body image. It can enrich a daughter's expectations regarding being treated by males in general. It also contributes to our daughters feeling more confident with a wide range of natural abilities. We can gather with other men getting honest about holding love, authority, and joy as we father our daughters. We can learn to accept the mystery of fathering, especially fathering daughters, allowing for the unfolding paternal apprenticeship.

Mentors

It is worth noting that deconstructing the glorified paternal projection does not preclude having a mentor. The difference is that in a genuine mentor relationship, the protegee is clear that she is giving the mentor a certain degree of power for her to be properly served. Secondly, she is willing to work with her fear that life will be unmanageable if she's not attached to someone allegedly larger than her. Diminishing the potency of this fear can occur if she is mindful that its origin was due to a compensation of inflated characteristics to the father because of maternal inaccessibility. Also helpful is remaining cognizant of the mentor's humanity which includes shortcomings. Rightful ownership of her power happens as she accepts responsibility to refine what she learns from her mentor. This refinement happens as her beliefs, intuition, and imagination bring the mentor's teachings to a deeper place within her, now emblematic of her vision and longing.

A healthy mentor relationship can easily slip into something a bit messier, with projections launched into the airways. There are just too many contributing variables, including each person's broken heart, the desire to be seen and chosen, a longing to have a dream being deemed as worthy, as well as one's gifts judged to be exemplary offerings for the world.

I like thinking that the mentor is the one most responsible for keeping the relationship honest and truly in the service of the mentee. However, if the mentee is an adult, she can obviously contribute to the discussion of keeping the relationship in service of her empowerment. Here are some questions that can help guide that process. After the mentee responds favorably to the teacher's charisma, does he reference her back to herself, her needs, curiosities, and values? Is there an opportunity for discussion about the role of projections in the relationship? Does the mentor encourage the mentee to explore other perspectives besides the one he provides? Does the mentor stay with open-ended questions, creating more room for the unfolding ethos of the mentee? Do the mentor and mentee remain clear about what they want from one another? Can they give themselves and one another permission to shamelessly stumble in the creation of their relationship? Is there clarity about when the mentor relationship needs to close?

Lastly, I want to acknowledge a daughter who genuinely experienced a father who was quite present, encouraging, and supportive. Curious enough, that daughter also runs the risk of generating an idyllic version of her paternal experience. However, rather than an inflated projection onto other males, these men may simply be viewed as inadequate, not measuring up to the wonderful father. Again, a daughter's loyalty defines her vision of her dad and of other men. And there's the daughter who is quite clear about her father's shortcomings. She may run the risk of inflating the darker side of her father and projecting it to other men. Ultimately, there is a significant psychological task facing a daughter regardless of her paternal experience.

Chapter 12

Being a Grown-up

"Being a grown-up must at the very least oblige a sense of total responsibility for our choices, their consequences, and for finding the courage to step into the perpetual demands life makes of us."

- *James Hollis* -

My hope is that you can appreciate how challenging being a grown-up is.

It's worth considering that most folks will shy away from embarking upon the arduous journey of adulthood. However, in doing so, they likely must turn against themselves and against life. The result is a life lacking meaning and depth and remaining a victim of the vicissitudes of fate and their inherent absurdity.

Unfortunately, one of my father's most valued offerings to me was his choice to turn against life and himself. I was 36 years old when I visited him in the hospital. I walked into his room to see a man's spirit atrophied, and his body emaciated, in a fetal position. Looking at me with forlorn eyes he said, "What do we do now, Paulie?" The only other exchange I recall was his uttering that he did not want to live, nor did he want to die. I had no idea what it meant for a man to be caught somewhere between life and death. I sat stunned and overwhelmed when the only option I could hold was to sit in silence with him. When he appeared to doze off, I quietly left. My father died four days later.

Almost 40 years have passed, and I remain only at the surface of understanding my father's life. "What do we do now, Paulie?" for me translates to "I made choices that got me somewhere I don't want to be." My best reflections upon these choices are that he was a Hero child from an alcoholic family and had no clue what it would mean to step away from that role. He was a self-identified alcoholic who was prone to seeing himself as a victim, as most alcoholics do. His essential worth remained just out of reach, afraid of living his gifts and susceptible to disdain for not seizing his own life.

My father had a large heart, he knew how to hold a large dream and remained lost regarding how he might bring life to his dreams. He likely witnessed one dream after another find its way to the place where dead dreams go to rest.

I will remain grateful for the two precious gifts he offered. The first is that last day we met in the hospital. Following his death, it didn't take long for me to realize that there was a hospital bed waiting for me, where I lay in defeat looking at my son and saying, "What do we do now, Jason?" If I wanted the ending to be different, then I would need to stop drinking, commit to living a self-examined life, know when to ask for help, know my own gifts and how they could best serve, and avoid being a victim by remaining generous and grateful. All of which was relatively easy to figure out, but very challenging to actually live. I still wonder if that is simply the way of it or is there an important message about me.

The second gift he offered me was modeling a deep sincere delight in the company of men. He loved telling stories, especially stories of a friend's triumph over adversity. He knew how to love men and call them to a celebration of life. As a result, I too, know how to love men and call them to an honoring of their path. Maybe these offerings are plenty, especially for a son whose father lost his way. Especially, when I remember that I too lose my way and if it were not for the guidance of mentors and support of friends, stepping out of adolescence may have remained elusive, with the path to elderhood remaining obscure and unattainable.

I tell this story because my father's challenge to be a grown-up, besides my own, has touched me very deeply. I'm not sure if anyone has ever explained how anyone gets on with the business of growing up. Sometimes, enough pain or loss will stop us from automatic living and begin to be curious about the options. Maybe seeing someone who talks and acts like an adult gets our attention. An old understanding of the word *maturity* is "in its proper time." I have come to believe that life will offer us numerous proper times to step into something larger than childhood. It may be some innocence, naivete, or a dependency being asked to die.

There will be inevitable distractions and impediments seducing us away from the work supporting what needs to die. So many dreams in childhood get broken. Why grow up and feel the anguish and dread of more shattered dreams? Why welcome adulthood when your parents were not real adults, therefore giving you no real map guiding maturation? And what about the idea that facing loss and challenges builds character? What is character and do we really need some? Aren't I big enough the way I am now? The excuses for not growing up are endless.

One reason to consider growing up is that I can't be myself if I stay somewhere I don't belong. There might be two indicators pointing me to where I belong. They are my wounds and my gifts. When we bring meaningful attention to both, some emerging adulthood is inevitable. Some curiosities supporting our wounds giving rise to living in a larger story include Have I been abused in some way? Have I been neglected? How are these injuries currently impacting my life? How do they shape the way I relate to others? Who might possess the medicine I need? Who might serve me as an ally in my healing? Can I accept being wounded without unnecessary self-diminishment?

The attention that can be brought to your gifts includes What are my gifts and strengths? Where do I go to have them further developed? Who might be an ally regarding their development? Who is unlikely to be supportive of their development? Am I willing to learn to carry my gifts as my calling to serve, rather than some testimony of being allegedly special? Am I willing to learn to carry my gifts such that they offer a robust contribution to my collaboration with others? Can I allow myself to learn and benefit from the gifts of others, without comparing them to mine?

I'm not so interested in growing up as a measure of character, as long as that suggests I am adapting to some external measure of adulthood. Rather, I want the notion of character to reflect the unique character that I am, my unique beliefs, values, and decisions, as well as the unique ways I have responded to fate's challenges and offerings. This understanding of character reflects how I have chosen to make meaning.

An old definition of the word *meaning* is "to name." We can name ourselves in endless ways, which include our roles, our unique characteristics, and our dreams. That's Part 1 of creating meaning. Part 2 is deciding how we will live the name we give ourselves. If you decide that you are intuitive, then what will it look like to fully live your intuition? The fullness of meaning typically calls for courage, accessing support, and getting honest as we assess how it is going.

There are 2 questions I recommend employing as meaning-makers. First, what is life asking for? Here are some responses to that question, none of which I ever find to be unusually cosmic or transcendent. Remain curious about where my gifts can best serve. Notice who walks with me and what they bring. Be aware of making excuses for those who bring little or nothing. Be grateful for those who bring much. Be conscious of what is out of my control. See what it is that you find seductive and what the seduction is asking from you. Be aware of situations calling for courage. Be mindful of how love is attempting to reach you.

Second, what is my soul asking of me? Here are some responses to this question. Name your longing. Accept what you fear. Accept what is out of your control. Remember where you come from. Notice a tendency to inflate or deflate. Be aware of walking away from yourself. Notice who in you awaits a welcome by you. Listen to your body. Be mindful of how you keep yourself in a small story.

Part 3 in making meaning is to accept what happens, when fate delivers something other than what you named and intended to manifest.

Meandering in Small Stories

Let's look at a number of ways adulthood can get delayed or seriously impaired - remaining in a small story. It's important to see growing up as living in a large soul story and not a large ego story. In his book, *Care for the Soul*, Thomas Moore offers, "Soul is not a thing, but a quality or a dimension of experiencing life and ourselves. It has to do with depth, value, relatedness, heart, and personal substance." Large soul stories reflect a receptivity for chaos, not as a dramatic agenda, but as a precursor to some form of creativity.

Large ego stories are typically quite worldly with some expression of generativity, achievement, or acquisition. These certainly may indicate that something of value is taking place but not necessarily reflective of a deepening maturity.

Impediments to Growing Up

Initiated into an illusion. Western culture's institutions initiate young people into a serious distortion of reality. There is a misrepresentation of life as understandable, predictable, and secure if you acquire the right education, the right job, marry the right spouse, live in the right neighborhood, practice the right religion, procure the right financial investments, and know the right people. These aspects of life certainly may generate a measure of comfort. However, they won't have us penetrating the essential mysteries of life such as love, courage, freedom, justice, and death, nor make life more predictable and secure. I hear stories regularly of people possessing socio-economic success and deeply confused about some tragic event befalling them as if education or a bank account could offer immunity to life's vicissitudes. Growing up becomes challenging when we are bewildered about how much depth of mystery and unpredictability characterizes the journey. Since there is allegedly the right action to perform, we live in the delusion we can get life right. We are not seeing life for what it is and therefore cannot accurately see ourselves as the ones living it. Such a distortion condemns us to a literalization of life shaped by various formulas like the ones listed above. It often takes the taste of defeat as our formulas fail to generate meaning, safety and a sustainable sense of depth.

Keeping some part of the self in exile. We don't come out of our families honoring all the different parts of ourselves. It simply would not have served a child's way of attempting to secure safety and love. Whatever we deemed unacceptable by our parents and/peers is likely to be relegated to some deplorable status. We may be mindful of this part, or it conveniently slid into the unconscious. One example of my own life is my mother with her eighth-grade education felt there was no need for formal education. I banished the student in me until I was a junior in college. Until then, I remained loyal to my mother in the hope she would not feel inadequate or intimidated by my education. I have worked with women who condemned their intelligence or their beauty to the land of the forgotten because they believed it made their fathers uncomfortable. We simply don't leave our families with all of ourselves. Growing up depends upon realizing who in you awaits your welcome and committing to offering that welcome. Internal marginalized parts of us tend to react to their marginalization like the way people who are disenfranchised. There is a tendency toward unrest and turbulence. These unwelcomed parts of us make immature decisions, react in ways that are counter-productive, sabotage what appears to operate well, become overdramatic, and are generally non-supportive of our rightful age. It can become quite obvious that someone seeking a greeting and integration is wanting our attention.

Keeping authority external. An old meaning of the word *authority* is "author or the one who causes growth." The hope regarding childhood is that the adults in our world are the ones causing growth and doing so with wisdom and compassion. Of course, that is not typically what happens. Many of my colleagues like to say that parents do the best they can. I like that, and it feels like half the story. Hence, I recommend parents do the best they can and it's not enough. I like this way of understanding the past even when I'm the parent in question. My inner authority began germinating when I decided to major in philosophy and was impressed with the work of Ludwig Feuerbach, a 19th-century German philosopher. One weekend in my junior year I returned home for a weekend and a sprout of inner authority sprang into the light. I announced to my Irish-Catholic family that I was now an atheist. My father promptly replied, "I don't give a shit what you are; when you're home, you'll go to church."

To which I countered with, "Okay, I guess that I won't be home much." I was deciding that my own philosophical beliefs would be defining my religious choices. My atheism lasted a decade or so. What really mattered was that the declaration of atheism was an act of leaving home. I am reminded of the theologian, Paul Tillich, suggesting that growing up was about

"Leaving home again, again and again." Not leaving home leaves the power of your growth with external authority figures.

Unconsciously reproducing or compensating for a family pattern. We survive childhood due to an ability to adapt and comply with family norms and rules. However, the decision to cope by acquiescing to the ethos of the family is not employed consciously. Hence, we take on a great deal that belongs to our parents without knowing it. Doug came to see me, reporting that marital issues brought him to my office. It wasn't long before it became apparent that Doug was spending quite a bit of time drinking with the guys. "How often do you get together with your male friends and have what you call 'a few beers'?" I asked, wondering if his wife's complaints might have any legitimacy.

"Once or twice per week. We get together at the local pub, shoot some pool or play cards," Doug reported, seemingly confident about the importance of his fraternizing.

"Do your friends ever come to the house, socializing with your wife and children?" I inquired, curious about how inclusive he was regarding connecting his friends with his family.

"No, no, the guys never come over," he intimated, suggesting that he was saying something he simply never considered.

"Tell me, how many guys are we talking about?" I questioned, wanting a better understanding of the level of connection he had with these men.

"Well, there's five of us. But, on most nights just four. Warren, Chuck, and Louie are the three I feel really close to," Doug described, his eyes brightening and cheeks softening.

"It sounds like you only interact with these guys on the designated pub nights. Has this been a pattern since you were married?" I wondered.

"No, heavens, I've been doing it forever. I mean isn't that what guys do? My father would surely be out twice per week with his buddies," he added, seeming to hope that his behavior somehow reflected a generic understanding of manhood.

"Did you ever meet your father's friends?" I asked, now wondering if he may have unconsciously reproduced a family pattern related to friendship.

Doug went on to describe one or two encounters with his father's friends. We began to explore the possibility that he unconsciously reproduced his father's way of engendering friendship and its impact upon his family. He decided to invite his friends to his home to watch a football game and made a point of telling his friends that his wife liked football which they thought was great. Gradually, Doug saw how much he took on his father's ritual of alcohol being a critical component when male friends gathered.

Judith and Frank came to my office reporting that they were struggling to be on the same page as they parented. It became clear they were each locked into *good cop–bad cop* respectively. I decided to postpone the question regarding if they could learn anything from the other person. Judith quickly made the point that she felt the need to balance Frank's harshness.

"Judith, tell me what would happen to the children if you didn't balance Frank's harshness?"

"Well, I don't know, it might hurt the kids; and who knows, they might even stop loving their dad," she added, her jaw tightening, the folds of her brow increasing.

"Judith, have you ever seen someone fathering like Frank?" I asked, wondering if she might be compensating when it came to holding authority.

"Yes, my father," she offered, with her eyes moistening.

"Did you fear your father?"

"I not only feared him, but I also don't like him to this day," she emphasized, moving from her chin raised in assertion to her face in her hands sobbing.

Over the next few sessions, Judith learned how much she

was compensating when holding authority with her children. She was desperately attempting to avoid what her father had created in her family of origin. She began to see that abdicating authority can create as much harm as abusing it. Little by little, she employed better boundaries with concrete consequences for unacceptable behavior. I was pleased to see how much Frank was willing to support her.

Fear of being too much or not enough. These fears tell the story of rightsizing ourselves. We can't grow up caught in a pattern of either oversizing or undersizing who we are. In both cases, we pretend to be someone we're not. When the fear of not being enough drives us, we get entangled in a knot of excessive striving. Such a campaign of efforting has us endlessly demonstrating we're enough. Of course, there's no arrival; our essential worth remains just out of reach. We literally can't be ourselves, because who we are is not here yet allegedly lying somewhere in the distant future. It is only too easy to slide into false modestly when the fear of being too much has a hold on us. When this happens, our gifts and strengths are minimized and not allowed to fully develop and be expressed. At the risk of overly gendering these fears, I have known many men afraid of not being enough and numerous women afraid of being too much. When either of these fears bears down upon us, remaining in connection to our personal worth becomes quite difficult.

Allowing a fractured dream to keep you hostage to disillusionment. An old mentor of mine would say, "Maturing depends upon dreaming, becoming deeply disillusioned and dreaming again." However, it is only too easy to turn against life and/or ourselves when a dream has shattered. It may be the death of a loved one, the end of a cherished relationship, the lack of reconciliation with a friend, or confidence is snuffed out due to some defeat. If we don't grieve and finally let go of a fractured dream, we allow disillusionment to condemn us to that place where hearts harden. We resent life for not cooperating or hold contempt for the fool who trusted life.

Unable to muster some measure of self-love. Over 40 years, the most prevalent declaration I've heard from clients is, "I really don't love myself." How does such a vital element of growing up escape so many? If we were treated unlovingly by early caregivers, then it's very easy to treat ourselves the way we were treated. We can also get caught up issuing disparaging thoughts and reflections about who we are when we make a mistake or fall short of meeting some expectation. The misguided thinking is that if we treat ourselves badly enough, then we won't reproduce unacceptable behavior. It is simply a bad way of treating ourselves when seeking change. It doesn't work.

Let's look more closely at how we might manage self-love more effectively. The first thing to notice is that either love for ourselves or for others is not mostly a feeling. Of course, a person may feel touched and reassured if you tell them you feel love for them. However, most of us are much more interested in how we are treated. I feel loved when I am understood, listened to, encouraged, accompanied, accepted, welcomed, and acknowledged. We can say that loving is acting in some loving way. It's the reason that affirmations don't' work. They tend to slide off the frontal lobe of the brain into the depths of lost memory. Again, we can see how trivial affirmations are when they are compliments given to another. At best, they offer a temporary feeling of being flattered and grateful.

Here are the 4 ingredients of *self-love* that I recommend: **humility**, **self-forgiveness**, **self-kindness**, and **openness to receive love from others**. We can understand humility as the gracious acceptance of our limitations. Humility helps us to make mistakes as a reflection of our participation in the human condition rather than a statement of inadequacy. Self-forgiveness helps restore our essential goodness. We accept that we will allow ourselves to be seduced away from what we hold dear and to be willing to repair a compassionate connection to ourselves through forgiveness. We're kind to ourselves when we respond to a need for rest, for food, for affiliation with others, for solitude, and for help. Lastly, we affirm love for ourselves by remaining open to the love being offered to us by others.

This business of growing up appears to need our honest attention. Without that, the ego remains convinced that it has already arrived at "grown up." The problem of course, is that there is no arriving at "grown up." The honest attention will call for an ever-unfolding measure of humility as the ego builds a seductive case for the accumulation of years being an alleged guarantee of maturity. The ego is constantly on the lookout for whatever can help it to feel valued, important, and secure.

Hence, the seduction of what I call **The 3 Amigos.**

The 3 Amigos

The words *sacred* and *seductive* do not commonly travel together. However, I've come to appreciate how the meanings of these words can contribute to a deepened resonance with the Self. 2 old meanings of the word *sacred* are "confirming what truly matters" and "to sacrifice." An old understanding of the word *seduction* is "to lead astray."

I worked in a semi-cloistered setting, seeing clients in my basement office for 35 years. The culture of my work was created by my values and my beliefs. With few exceptions, there were minimal situations asking me to question my integrity, or how I held power, or how effective my work was. As there were few challenges, I felt comfortable holding the authority to confirm I was enough.

Very little was "calling me astray" from taking responsibility for my own worth. However, it was like starting to work out at the gym several times per week, lifting 5 pounds for a triceps kick-back exercise. Then deciding to continue to lift 5 pounds over the next 3 months. It sounds like a comfortable situation, with no real strengthening taking place. I would be taking up residency in a very contracted understanding of body building and strength. An honest awareness of my strength could only take place if I felt the lure of lifting heavier weight, discovering it was either too much or a good fit.

Analogous to the gym workouts is how we measure our inner authority and responsibility to confirm we are enough. We can either remain cloistered lifting 5 pounds repeatedly or give the authority away to what seductively calls to us. A key will be a commitment to remain mindful of what we empower to call us away from ourselves. What can lead us astray does so because of the power we give it. This is a significant understanding to hold regarding the nature of seduction.

Giving away Personal Authority

Let's look at 3 popular recipients of our authority. I have come to believe that the most important spiritual responsibility is to maintain authority over our essential goodness, or the belief that we are enough. Such a belief is the bedrock of inner authority and growing up. 4 years ago, I was called out of my basement dwelling and discovered 3 sources of seduction, with the power of leading me astray from holding inner authority.

The 3 recipients - **The 3 Amigos** - are **greed**, **vanity**, and **power**. They each possess the ability to masquerade as genuine declarations of my being enough. Of course, like any bogus source of power, we must return to the trough repeatedly, attempting to quench an insatiable thirst for feeling good enough. The hope is we discover that these alleged three resources cannot hold the authority for our essential goodness.

Let's look more closely at these 3 sirens. An old understanding of the word *greed* is "glutenous or ravenous," meaning to devour feverishly, knowing no limits. Greed is not limited to money, it can include fame, prestige, and recognition. Greed can't confirm we are enough since its essence abolishes limits and it can offer a delusionary sense of security. The notion of "enough" has no meaning under the auspices of greed. An old meaning of the word *vanity* is "empty." It translates into an attachment to looking good. Such an attachment condemns a person to skin-deep metrics of personal worth. Vanity guarantees that any authentic expression of being enough will remain empty, excluding one's character and intelligence. Of all the clients with whom I have worked, those considered to be beautiful women struggle the most to have a felt sense of their personal value. The ability to receive immediate confirmation of how one looks can be a luring substitute for being truly known and appreciated both by others and by oneself.

An ancient definition of the word *power* is "able to," allegedly able to do whatever is required or desired. Like greed, demonstrations of power have an inexhaustible quality to them. They demand evidence that "being able" still exists. Worse yet, demonstrate that their next display will far exceed the prior one. What makes unbridled power dangerous is that it can cloak all feelings of vulnerability and insecurity. We can ask what does it mean to confirm the sacred while experiencing the temptation of one or more of these enticements?

The Price Tag

We can pretend we possess an immunity to these irresistible allures; but until we mindfully see the potency of greed, vanity, and power, we're only fooling ourselves, and suffering the consequences of their incantations.

Here are several of these unfortunate results:

- There is a loss of personal power. As greed, vanity or power define you, you no longer hold authority over your own self-definition. What is so insidious is that it can be extremely difficult to see that one of the amigos holds power and you don't. Genuine personal power means you create an honest and compassionate relationship with endeavoring to hold your personal worth, your vulnerability, and feelings of insecurity.
- Because these 3 cannot satisfy the soul's need to value itself, you are condemned to an insatiable quest for more. Such questing cannot find a peaceful place to rest in fullness.
- The drive for more translates into developing a myopic vision, which can blind you to what is truly sustainable such as compassion, integrity, gratitude, and intimacy.
- Decision-making is compromised as it becomes challenging to hold a larger vision, considerable important elements related to decision making.
- The obsession generates exhaustion mitigating your ability to be fully alive.
- Because of the loss of power to define oneself, it becomes a chore to define relationships. There's confusion about how to participate in a relationship, what is desired and what one wants to offer.

Given how many times we are told we're wrong, inadequate, mistaken, unqualified and undeserving, it calls for fortitude and a devotion to avoid allowing **The 3 Amigos** to massage a psychc longing to be regarded and respected. It takes a great deal of psychological muscle to continue to claim the authority to confirm that you are enough. Come to know these 3 seductions and you come to know yourself. Come to know how receptive you are to their influences, and you come to know your strength. Their power simply comes from your unwillingness to commit to the heavy lifting it takes to hold the authority that deems you enough.

Working with the Sacred

How can surrendering to the stupor of a seduction become an opportunity for the sacred? We are working with the first old definition of the word *sacred*, "confirming what truly matters." First, it truly matters that you can have a felt sense of having surrendered the authority of your essential worth to greed, vanity, or power. Nothing empowers your relationship to your personal worth more than knowing you have stepped away from it. Secondly, you are on a deeply sacred path or confirming what truly matters when you recommit to the stewardship of your goodness.

Here are some recommended steps when calling for the sacred during a seduction:

Exercising compassionate mindfulness. This is a state of awareness that either you are in the grips of seduction or about to be. The key is to hold your knowing with compassion rather than berate yourself for allegedly being weak.

Remembering. Recall that being seduced is more about participation in the human condition rather than about you. It helps to remember that greed, vanity, and power only have as much potency as you give them.

Curiosity. Be curious about how you can interrupt your attachment to the source of seduction. It helps to acknowledge how little these temptations can bring to you. It's especially beneficial to hold the seductive process as simply a call back to yourself.

Process with trusted others. It is extremely helpful to shamelessly talk about where you feel vulnerable to a particular seduction, especially with those also willing to get honest about their adventures with temptation.

Allow The Amigos to offer a reminder of what truly matters. Feeling seduced by power can remind you there's nothing else to prove. I find it helpful to recall that power can easily go disguised as a spiritual endeavor. I find myself no longer interested in being evolved as long as that implies in any way, that I no longer need to attend to the task of being an ordinary man. Seduced by vanity reminds you of your internal and external beauty. Seduced by greed reminds you that you have enough, and you are enough.

Be willing to sacrifice. Employ the second old definition of the word *sacred* - "to sacrifice" - and be willing to sacrifice the placebo offered by one or more of **The Amigos.** Of course, the challenge is that the seductions offer both an immediate high and illusion of control. The ego basks in the fantasy of being able to do whatever. Working with the mantra "I do a lot, I make a lot, I acquire a lot, therefore I am a lot" can gradually nudge an attachment to greed or power out of the unconscious. Obviously, the more conscious you are of the three amigos the more freedom you have to work with them. Enhancing your freedom occurs when the seduction of power is interrupted by loosening your grip upon an attachment to be right or correct. Others typically feel free to offer diverse perspectives as you hold more curiosity than alleged certainty.

Diminish the attachment to your gifts. Your gifts represent how you can likely best serve. However, the darker side of your relationship with your gifts can be a fascination of how much they can do, how much notoriety they bring. Once you fall victim to the illusion that you are simply your gifts, one of **The Amigos** is likely holding authority over your personal worth.

You will walk away from yourself, stepping away from the authority to support your essential goodness. The only issues are how far will you walk and if you will wake up enough to see the distance traveled. Such rambling is neither pathological nor an aberration of the human condition. It simply is the nature of the journey. We naturally become charmed by the promises offered by vanity, greed, and power. Much more harm is created by pretending we have not walked away from ourselves. We can get consumed by a seduction, not aware of how far we have drifted away nor clear about how to get home.

Being mindful of a seductive allure is an opportunity to confirm what truly matters. You can fervently hold the task of substantiating you are enough, no matter how difficult it may be. An old meaning of the word *prayer* is "an earnest request or petition." Our prayer or request may be for enough mindfulness, grace, and humility needed to see a seductive spell, interrupt its hold, and return to ourselves. We can live in such a prayer, knowing we are up to the business of confirming what truly matters and supporting the odyssey of growing up.

Your growing up happens in the proper time when you can pause and offer consideration to which impediment or amigo has your attention. Most of all, be gentle with yourself. Growing up is about dying and birthing, both deserving tenderness and care. I strongly encourage you not to see growing up as an act of improvement. Such a vision condemns who you are now to be unworthy. Growing up is about deepening and strengthening your ability to honor the depth and uniqueness of who you are. Feel free to improve your ability to fix a broken door or change the oil in your vehicle. But stay away from bringing any paradigm of improvement to your soul.

Chapter 13

Becoming Relational

"Owning our own story can be hard but not nearly as difficult as spending our lives running from it. Embracing our vulnerabilities is risky but not nearly as dangerous as giving up on love and belonging and joy – the experiences that make us the most vulnerable. Only when we are brave enough to explore the darkness will we discover the infinite power of our light."

- Brené Brown -

We learn a great deal about being relational in our families of origin, mostly driven by the modeling offered and our eagerness to learn how to love. We may later forget about the importance of love; but in those early years that's what we want to know. Some of our interest is based upon a yearning to reproduce the oneness we experienced in the womb. Another motivation is simply a desire to survive. If we can demonstrate we are lovable and loving, then we are giving the clan the best reason we have for sustaining our inclusion and our place in the group. However, I increasingly believe we know on some level that love is what life is all about. It is the raison d'etre.

We'll be exploring what it means to become more relational, which is a large inquiry. For now, let's say that becoming more relational means connecting to others while remaining connected to ourselves. That's what we will look at - how to stay connected to ourselves while building connections to others and, of course, distilling some meaning about these connections to ourselves and others.

The status of boundaries in a family offers a great deal of material regarding what love means and how connections to others and self will be organized. As we saw earlier, some level of enmeshment in a system declares that love is a devotion to the welfare of the group, particularly the needs and feelings of others. On the other hand an Estranged Family defines love as support for the independence and autonomy of the self. Separation is not perceived as a loss, but rather as an opportunity for everyone to do their own thing.

I am regularly amazed at how often couples bring these two different versions of love to their relationship. Breakdowns often happen because the enmeshed partner claims there's not enough together time. While the estranged partner complains that his or her freedom to pursue individual interests is not being honored. Learning and healing can occur if each person can realize how much the boundaries in their early family life defined love and being relational. If they can see that the connection to self and the connection to the other both make valuable contributions to the relationship, then an opportunity is created to live into a larger love story.

Reproducing & Compensating

We come out of either an Enmeshed or an Estranged Family, and then reproduce or compensate for where we come from. When folks from an enmeshed system compensate, they create a family that employs the large boundaries of an Estranged Family, attempting to offer care for individuals as opposed to stressing care for others. When people from an estranged system compensate, they create a family employing more permeable boundaries, therefore stressing the care for others.

We all carry 2 fears into any committed relationship - the fear of abandonment and the fear of consumption. One fear is dominant while the other is inferior. Typically, being raised in an Enmeshed Family has us bringing the fear of abandonment to a committed relationship while coming out of an Estranged Family has us carrying a fear of consumption. The former fears losing others while the latter fears losing the self.

Let's look at the 4 options taking place as folks from an Enmeshed Family connect with someone from an Estranged Family. Curious enough, it does occur quite often that people from different types of families come together.

	Enmeshed	**Estranged**
1.	Reproduce	Reproduce
2.	Reproduce	Compensate
3.	Compensate	Reproduce
4.	Compensate	Compensate

What happens with these varying combinations of reproducing or compensating for the boundaries of the system we came from?

Option 1. A person from an Enmeshed Family is wanting to reproduce their familiar permeable boundaries, likely carrying an abandonment fear. The partner is reproducing his or her familiar non-permeable boundaries, likely carrying a dominant consumption fear or fear of losing the self. A popular dance ensues where the person from the enmeshed system steps forward in pursuit of the partner while the partner from the Estranged Family steps back. Such a relationship soon becomes tedious as no one really gets their needs met. Of course, it is only too easy to decide that the person from the Enmeshed Family is trying to build a meaningful relationship while the person from the Estranged Family is sabotaging the process by distancing. A more accurate and possibly more compassionate view of the distancing partner is that he or she is simply employing physical or psychological distance in order to attain a necessary boundary to support their understanding of love which is care for the self.

Emotional intimacy is only possible if this approach–avoid dance is interrupted. The partner from the Estranged Family needs to learn to employ more sophisticated boundaries, simply starting with saying "no" and "yes" authentically. Folks from the Enmeshed Family need to learn to choose themselves. They do that by allowing their lives to be guided by their desire, being careful not to fall prey to the self-indictment of selfishness. It is also important to develop an active support system, so they have multiple ways of getting their emotional needs met. They might also engender their own spiritual path. They are learning to deepen their care for the self.

Option 2. Here the enmeshed partner is reproducing where he or she comes from, while the partner is compensating for their early estranged experience. They are both prioritizing care for the other, with self-betrayal likely being present. This arrangement can be seen as merger, fusion, or co-dependency. Each person needs to get their own life as depicted in the first example with the reproduction of enmeshment.

Option 3. In this example, the partner from enmeshment is compensating and the partner from estrangement is reproducing where they come from. This configuration constitutes the classic estranged relationship. This couple can be content living thousands of miles away from one another with periodic rendezvous. If they wish to create an emotionally intimate relationship with depth, they will need to trade in distancing as their preferred boundary and learn to say "yes" and "no" authentically and learn to show up for the other offering care and encouragement for the partner's emotional needs.

Option 4. This alternative is like the first. It is an approach-avoid dance, with the enmeshed partner doing the avoidance and the estranged partner approaching. The compensating enmeshed partner needs to employ more effective boundaries replacing distancing while the estranged partner needs to lean into more self-care. The approach–avoid dance can be interrupted if the approaching partner learns how to choose oneself, while the avoiding partner learns to let go of using distancing as a boundary and employ boundaries that support a real connection to the other.

It helps to unpack the notion of committing to a relationship. It is worth considering that it might entail remaining curious about where we come from, especially the prevailing definition of love reflected in that early family. We can notice either reproducing or compensating for our initial exposure to boundaries. There will inevitably be a measure of mystery surrounding how we approach self-care and care for another.

It is worth considering that becoming relational is both a call to togetherness, shared values, adventures, tasks, and learning as well as a summons to honor unique individual strengths, dreams, interests, and desires. There is no way to achieve a perfect balance of connecting to yourself and connecting to your partner or friend. We can only remain corrective by asking: Is there too much of me in the relationship? Is there too little of me in the relationship? Is there too much connection to the other?

The last question can appear antithetical to becoming relational. When there's too much connection to the other (enmeshment), there's not enough connection to yourself. Without enough of you participating, the relationship engine runs on half of its cylinders. A robust relational dynamic depends upon both people contributing their desires, beliefs, and dreams to the fabric of the relationship. Only when both people bring what truly matters to them, is some form of deepening possible.

What is Depth?

The word *depth* comes from the word *deep* as in "the deep seas." We can say that a relationship has depth if what goes on between them happens somewhere beneath the surface, in the deep sea of the self. People and events tangential to those folks encountering one another can be viewed as happening on the surface. We can relate to one another the way a typical disc jockey speaks on the radio, filling the airways with meaningless chatter. Of course, in our extroverted culture, an abundance of language is often seen as having some measure of meaning rather than simply drawing the curtain and calling verbosity for what it is. If communication does not relate to what people define as really mattering, then they are likely skimming the surface.

Sometimes what really matters is not spoken about but lived. I am thinking of the play I enjoy with my son and several of my friends. The laughter, the jocularity and spontaneity become a lived testimony of affection, freedom, joy, love and appreciation - all things we define as really mattering. What really matters does not need to be cloaked in severity. I'm aware that I also experience depth when witnessing something said or enacted that is true for that person accompanied by compassion. Depth often reflects meaning and an old understanding of the word *meaning* is "to name." When we name ourselves with language reflecting our values, what and who we love, and what we cherish, there is depth and meaning.

When my granddaughter turned 13, I thought it might

be appropriate to bring more depth and meaning to our relationship. We had just returned home from an evening at the theatre and decided to jump into the hot tub before closing out the day. I turned to Erika and said, "I see how important friendship is for you these days," knowing all too well that friendship was something that truly mattered to her.

"Oh yes, grandpa. It is extremely important to me," she beamed, not withholding her enthusiasm for her peers.

"Okay then, how would you define a good friend?" I asked, confident that she would take the question seriously.

"Grandpa, that's a very difficult question," she offered, lifting her head from a bowed posture of quiet inquiry.

"Yes, I know it is and it's an important question. So, let's start by asking this. When you fly to Miami with your father, what does the flight attendant tell you to do with the oxygen mask?"

"I know she tells me to do something with the mask, but I can't remember," she admitted, squinting her eyes and leaning forward.

"Well, she tells you to put the mask on yourself first before helping another person," I noted, wondering where she might take the information.

After several pondering quiet moments with her arms flailing out of the water sending liquid everywhere, she screamed, "I'm not living that way!"

"Honey, no problem, you've got time," I replied, pleased that she was able to process the metaphor from the oxygen mask story and obviously understood the importance of self-care in a friendship.

Our encounter had depth as it reflected the primacy of friendship in Erika's life and the richness of her intention to be a good friend. There was also an implied devotion to learn more about friendship, indicated by the water dripping off my head.

Emotional Intimacy

I think of Emotional Intimacy as the unity of two separate and unique individuals accompanied by some measure of depth and compassion. The unity reflects the best of enmeshment while the separate and unique expresses the best of estrangement. The element of depth signifies something other than casual, and compassion denotes a measure of heartful participation.

Feelings of love appear to be a relatively natural expression of the human condition, while Emotional Intimacy must be learned. Unfortunately, many folks attempt to create an emotionally intimate relationship simply based upon loving feelings, which is a setup for failure. Emotional Intimacy remains a daunting topic for most couples. It is either reduced to feelings of love or to sexuality. Both topics are certainly worth considering but Emotional Intimacy cannot be reduced to one or to both. It can be helpful when exploring emotional intimacy to be clear about a worthwhile starting point.

My hunch is that Karen Horney, a neo-freudian analyst, gave us an important place to begin the inquiry. She suggested that we develop three coping mechanisms in childhood, which remain with us throughout life. These coping skills are **adaption**, **domination**, and **distancing -** all of which are meant to support our safety in childhood. These ways of managing challenges are not designed to help build intimate rapport. When adaption is employed in a relationship, the person adapting merges with the other. They don't bring their desires, beliefs, and values to the relationship. In a way, we can say that the adapting person is not really participating in the relationship, they are an extension of the other. As mentioned earlier, domination mostly occurs through an attachment to being right or winning. Domination is designed to limit the other's participation in the relationship. Distancing either physically or emotionally limits the participation of both people. A key way to begin building Emotional Intimacy is to notice what one of the three coping styles is your favorite and interrupt it as a primary way to relate to your partner.

The next step is to commit to building both self-trust and making yourself trustworthy. I'm fond of the operational definition of *trust* used in early experiments regarding trust. *Trust* was defined as two beliefs, the belief that I will tell you the truth and the belief that I will treat you kindly. If your partner holds both beliefs, then we say that he or she trusts you or finds you to be trustworthy. Self-trust is equally important. I trust myself if I believe I will allow myself to know my own truth and treat myself kindly. When working with a couple, I'm primarily interested in how each of them is doing trusting themselves. Most folks find it to be a novel topic; and, as I spell it out, they become willing to address it.

The most common question is: What does it mean to believe I will allow myself to know my own truth? I point out that it means you will prioritize knowing your desire, knowing how you feel emotionally, knowing what you believe and value, and knowing where you come from (your early family experience). I go on to suggest that you will believe that you will treat yourself kindly when you eat while hungry, rest when tired, contact a friend when needing affiliation, ask for what you want and need, and say "no" and "yes" authentically.

As your self-trust and your trustworthiness build, you can begin to focus on bringing more of your emotional needs to the relationship. Here's a list of emotional needs: receiving undivided attention, feeling heard, feeling understood, feeling trusted, feeling accepted, feeling encouraged, feeling appreciated, feeling loved, feeling desired, receiving affection and nurturance, feeling chosen, feeling invited into collaboration, wanting to be forgiven rather than accused and blamed, expecting committed participation during a relational breakdown, and feeling comforted especially during challenging times. It is extremely common for folks to simply not know what their emotional needs are. When it is unlikely in childhood that emotional needs will be met, the best way to cope is to repress the needs which anesthetizes any possible feelings of rejection or hurt. The result is that we believe we don't have any emotional needs. I recommend placing a list of emotional needs on the refrigerator door, which is not an indictment of anyone's intelligence. It simply denotes the arduous work of pulling an emotional need out of the land of repression.

Episodic Intimacy vs. Committed Intimacy

I believe that New Age thinking has the tendency to mitigate many of the challenges inherent to the human condition. Consequently, what I call Episodic Intimacy has become quite popular. Let's look more closely at the difference between Episodic Intimacy and Committed Intimacy. Each which can happen between friends, spouses, partners, extended family and colleagues.

There are at least two expressions of Emotional Intimacy, with one gaining increasing popularity. Episodic Intimacy is becoming more and more in vogue. It can offer some advantages that don't come with the territory of Committed Intimacy. It allows participants the chance to avoid the inevitable messy conditions of Committed Intimacy. The mess refers to conflict, diverse beliefs and values, the need to develop agreements that support the employment of non-blameful accountability, and the need to competently employ boundaries that support an individual's autonomy while not fracturing rapport with the other.

Episodic Intimacy

- There is typically a large number of folks referred to as "friends." This is easily accomplished since the work, time, and energy needed to support Committed Intimacy isn't required.

- Episodes or events constitute the basic medium of connection. Taking initiative can occur; but, even then, participants are clear that the meeting does not reflect a commitment to build something meaningful. There may simply be joy in an occasional meeting.
- Participants employ time elapsing and physical distance as needed boundaries. There is no need to develop boundaries that truly serve the deepening of the relationship.
- The episode is often comprised of accounts of experiences with third parties and events tangential to the relationship.
- Positive feelings constitute the connective tissue for the participants. These feelings evolve from shared beliefs and values. There may also be genuine joy and welcome in receiving each other. Diverse beliefs and values are not typically addressed.
- There is little or no focus or communication about what participants actually want from one another. When we want something from someone and we tell them, we move into a deeper level of intimacy. Episodic participants may not be ready or willing to move there.
- Conflict is not typically engaged in by the participants. In fact, in the name of "we have so much in common," avoidance is the rule of the day. Conflict belongs to the messiness of committed intimacy.
- The relationship is not typically defined as a container for individual or collective growth. Shared

time is the priority as well as the intention to create shared time. For the most part, time together is defined as a "feel-good time."

- Men are particularly susceptible to being limited to Episodic Intimacy due to the cultural prohibition placed upon them regarding living from their heart.
- Participants often focus on offering historical updates rather than current life experiences.
- Magic tends to lace the vision of the relationship. There is a tendency to distort and inflate just how close the participants are in the relationship. It's just not so easy to admit to ourselves or to the other person that we are engaged in a lighter version of intimacy. I believe that this kind of honesty can be helpful and support being in integrity. We can simply give ourselves the freedom to engage in different levels of intimacy rather than making one type sacred and the other unfortunate.

Committed Intimacy

- The relationship is defined as a container for the growth of the participants as well as the relationship. Participants remain open to feedback regarding personal focuses such as: self-sabotage, levels of transparency, the expression of emotion and desire, accountability, what is given and received in the relationship, exploration of how people are loving and being loved, expressed curiosity about what the relationship may be asking for, the quality of collaboration related to tasks undertaken, attention to how they relate to money, exploration of the spiritual dimension of the relationship.

- There is an ongoing invitation to actively participate in one another's lives. There is an invitation to undertake adventures, seminars and workshops, play, sex, dates, vacations, and work.
- There are ongoing requests regarding what participants want from one another. When I ask couples if they are making requests of one another, they either have a blank look on their faces or ask, "What kind of requests?" It's only too easy to bring the expectation that our parents will know what we need into our adult relationships. I have heard repeatedly, "He or she should know what I need." Disappointment prevails when I say, "No they shouldn't." Actively making requests allows the desire to have a voice and possibly reach satisfaction. They also support resolution when someone has an unmet need.
- Participants are committed to engaging in conflict by avoiding the dynamics of "win-lose" and "right-wrong," and continuing to learn to refine their confrontational skills. It's very helpful to accept that learning to support relational breakdowns is a lifelong task.
- Participants welcome both shared beliefs and diverse ones. When there is a genuine commitment to be emotionally intimate, then the evolving uniqueness of each person will present diverse beliefs, desires, and values. There will be plenty of opportunities to learn how to support and learn from encountering diversity with the people we love.
- Participants commit to employing boundaries that support each person's individuation as well as the quality of depth and meaning of the relationship.

Relationships might reflect a bit from each paradigm. Episodic connections certainly can serve folks living at a great distance from one another. They provide an opportunity to catch up, reminisce, and remain in one another's life. Committed Intimacy allows you to go somewhere no one goes alone. It provides opportunities for growth, relational skill-building, and creating a bond lending itself to depth and meaning. What is important is to be clear and intentional about what kind of relationship is desired. Couples often slide into Episodic Intimacy without knowing it took place.

Here are some questions that can help guide the decision-making process: Do I enjoy giving to this person? Do I want to know this person better? Does this person appear to make desirable offerings to me? Is this person curious about me? Do we have a strong level of compatibility? Do I want to explore something more episodic with this person? Or do I have the time and energy to build a Committed Intimacy with this person?

If these questions raise some level of longing for you, then you may be ready to explore a connection that is more committedly intimate. Even if they raise fear, you may simply be identifying a developmental edge that has been waiting for you. You may also allow Episodic Intimacy to offer you a wide range of intimate experiences.

Psychological Regression

Once you decide upon the journey of a Committed Intimacy, you will certainly have a myriad of experiences, one being psychological regression. It can be the biggest obstacle to Committed Intimacy. It is the temporary loss of your adult capacity to think clearly, feel emotions with stability and resiliency, and act in a constructive manner. Instead, thinking, feeling, and behaving become more indicative of a younger version of you.

It's too easy to reduce an understanding of regression to "You're not acting your age." That may be true, and a more healing perspective might be "A younger version of you is looking for your attention." Unconsciously acting out from a regressed place can be unfortunate and even tragic. Violating another's boundaries, abruptly leaving a relationship, suicide and homicide are often the results of unconscious psychological regression. Certainly, most relationship breakdowns are due to regression taking place with little or no mindfulness of what is happening or knowing what to do about it.

Indicators of Regression

Let's look more closely at when indications of regression are taking place:

Verbosity or dead silence. Excessive talking is usually a way to argue or fight. The chatter is an attempt to either prove you're right or win, or it may be simply an attack on the other's character. Silence may reflect the nervous system's need for flight or freeze, indicating that the psyche is on survival mode.

Almost a complete inability to identify what is needed or wanted. Younger versions of us simply don't have enough capacity for significant introspection to accurately identify the nature of support that would be helpful.

Extreme thinking. A common use of language includes terms like *everyone, no one, always, never,* and *every time*. This kind of black and white thinking makes it very difficult to summon enough discernment and discretion to support clear decision-making. A common consequence is behavior that is both unfortunate and even self-sabotaging.

Loss of options. When regression is moderate to high, you will either decide that you have one alternative or none. If the regression is low, two options might be recognized. Feeling fear is heightened during a regressive state. Because children typically associate a lack of safety with feeling scared, it's common during regression to feel both scared and unsafe. That puts you in a place of coping for survival and when that happens there is little or no hope to engage that part of the brain that generates creative vision.

A tendency to create a single, rigid interpretation of what is currently happening. As the need for safety increases so do our defenses and rigid thinking regarding what will provide adequate safety. There is very little opportunity in regression to consider various ways of seeing the situation.

A dysregulated nervous system. It can be very difficult to regulate a nervous system during a regressive episode. Dysregulation is accompanied by spontaneous perspiration, cold hands, dry mouth, and shallow breathing. It can also be said that the previous characteristics of regression also indicate the likelihood of nervous system dysregulation.

An acute sense of urgency. There is often a pressing need to speak or act. The regressive thinking behind the urgency usually has something to do with feeling unsafe, although there is no sign of an unfolding crisis.

Working with Psychological Regression

Working ourselves out of a psychological regression means returning to what appears to be adult thinking, feeling, and acting accompanied by feelings of safety. Of course, a major challenge is that when most adults are regressed, they simply deny it. A key is to see regression as normal and as an opportunity to attend to the needs of a younger part of ourselves.

Let's look at several helpful steps regarding returning to adulthood:

Education. Getting educated about psychological regression is critical. We can't interrupt something if we don't know it's happening. Unriddled regression can take place at home and at work, seriously jeopardizing what's important to us. Our initial awareness about a regressive episode may only come hours later or the next day. Let that be okay. Eventually, with practice, you will be mindful of regression while it is happening and then able to interrupt it. I recall several years ago I was arguing with my wife in our kitchen. As she turned and walked away, I began to yell, "I'm 6, I'm 6." She returned to the kitchen looking at me as if I had lost it. I told her the good news, which took her a few minutes to appreciate.

Get socially engaged. We hear so much about fight, flight, and freeze, losing sight of social engagement as the nervous system's first preference for support and safety. By social engagement, I don't mean some casual relationship, but one based upon trust, compassion, and honesty. When you know you're regressed, call a friend, mentor, or clergyperson whom you trust.

Identify the original story. Typically, regression feels like the repeat of a childhood story. It is likely that in the original story you were not able to say and do what would have felt empowering, authentic, and safe. The original players are often authority figures or some bullies at school. With the support of a trusted other, imagine telling the person who criticized you, hurt you, or in some way neglected you exactly what their treatment of you makes you feel. Let yourself be angry, sad, hurt, and scared. See if you can allow yourself to feel these emotions in your body and express them with as much passion as needed without hurting yourself or the environment. Let the child in you who was hurt in the original story know that you will protect him or her to the best of your ability. This kind of support is likely what the younger version of you needed and did not get. Offering it now can be healing and may mitigate a need for future regressions around this particular issue. It may be helpful to hear some encouraging words from your ally, asking him or her for what you need. Most of all, let the younger versions of you know that you have their back. You can then further regulate your nervous system by closing your eyes and calling to mind a very peaceful and tranquil scene. Stay with the image for 30 seconds or so and then let the image go and begin to track internal sensations such as tightness in the throat, pulsation over the eyes, butterflies in the stomach, or heaviness in the legs.

Continue tracking these sensations until you notice a strong sense of calm coming over your body. It is critical to appreciate that addressing regression is mostly not about dealing with anybody in the world. It is a time to firm up a loving and supportive connection with younger versions of ourselves.

Pulling the historical weight off the current person to whom you are reacting. Your perceptions and reactions can change dramatically when you separate the historical figures from the current ones. You may find that you are not quite as reactionary with less of an emotional charge. That doesn't necessarily mean you have no issue with the current person. You might have one and it will likely be more manageable.

No matter what kind of family we are raised in, the process of growing up will be arduous work. It is not a task that ends in some cozy fashion. It is a lifelong odyssey requiring learning how to live with life's mystery, unpredictability, and insecurity. My wish is that you will notice who possesses the capacity to help and support you. Do what you can to hold the faith that such resources exist and do your best at identifying and accessing them. You deserve to be gifted with what they have to offer, and later you will be asked to make similar offerings.

Chapter 14

Addressing Relational Breakdowns

"Anybody can become angry, that is easy; but to be angry with the right person, and to the right degree, and at the right time, and for the right purpose, and in the right way, that is not within everybody's power, that is not easy."

- Aristotle -

Most of us come from families where there was simply inadequate instruction and poor modeling regarding what to do when there is a breakdown between two people. Breakdowns refer to folks not feeling heard or understood. Someone might feel blamed or falsely accused. Possibly, a breakdown occurs because someone feels forgotten or excluded. They also happen when someone feels hurt or used; and sometimes, they are the result of people holding different needs or beliefs and values. There are numerous contributions to something happening between people that feel contentious and troublesome. There are 2 predominant responses to an upset. The first is avoidance and the second is a power struggle.

Let's look more closely at what happens when avoidance is employed. Avoidance takes place when the person who is upset avoids bringing their feelings to other family members when family members are directly involved with the issue.

Avoidance can also take place when family members view a member as carrying some level of tension or angst and they simply stay clear of that individual. Several unfortunate patterns ensue when avoidance is the chosen protocol for dealing with relationship problems.

When issues are swept under the rug the dust of passive aggression sweeps through the household. Passive aggression is the unconscious expression of anger. Classic examples include forgetting about an agreement, procrastinating, responding with silence, taking everything too personally resulting in claims of being victimized, resisting problem-solving and collaboration, becoming more exclusive and non-welcoming, as well as distancing and withdrawing. Avoidance can also result in unpredictable explosive behavior as piles of issues build eventually becoming volcanic. There is also what's been labeled as "gunny sacking," which is the refusal to address a current breakdown by focusing only upon some past event.

The second approach to breakdowns is the tendency to get into power struggles. These encounters are driven by participants being motivated by either the need to be right and/or to win. Although there is plenty of action, people do not feel heard, understood, and resolved. The nuanced truth is that no one truly wins. The alleged winner will likely be the recipient of passive aggression by the alleged loser. A common reaction to ongoing power struggles is simply resigning oneself to the impossibility of reaching resolution and slipping quietly into avoidance.

The key is to be willing to track attachments to be right or to win. Only then is there a possibility to letting them go. However, releasing a need to be right is no easy task. It's only too easy to feel threatened, to feel some impending loss while in the fray of a relational breakdown. It could be the direction taken to parent children, how to spend money, how to decide where to vacation, how to decorate the home, where to go for dinner, or a major decision at work. There is a strong tone of

"You're either with me or against me." When we have never witnessed or experienced a breakdown without someone losing, it's just too easy to be convinced that some measure of loss is inevitable. It will take a considerable leap of faith to believe that loss is not at all necessary.

If you're willing to take on your attachment to being right or to win, be aware; you will then be opening to deeper parts of yourself. The good news is that you will be taking the first real steps toward being an authentic peacemaker. Such an identity is a large undertaking, and extremely honorable. It may never be generally known how much peace you bring to what transpires in your kitchen as well as exchanges with friends and colleagues. Hence, such peacemaking can be quite humbling. There will be no Noble Prize awarded to those making kitchen-peace.

Releasing a desire to be right calls for steadfast attention and listening to what happens in your interior world. You will be greeted by the parts of yourself dwelling just behind the need to be right. You may meet someone confused, uncertain, or even mistaken. Of course, there's often someone quite scared, afraid of feeling inadequate or unlovable. There's the anticipation of loss if you're not right, the loss of being perceived unfavorably or some option losing its credibility. Essentially, being a peacemaker means remaining curious about who lives on the other side of the drive to be right. It also means being compassionate with whom you find there since it's likely to be someone feeling vulnerable.

Hopefully, it's somewhat obvious that to make peace with others, we need to make peace with ourselves. The more we are mindful of what is true about us, the more options we have regarding relating to others. We can be curious about what the other is saying, rather than quickly disagreeing. We are able to listen, acknowledge and notice what is resonating for us. We can respond with a level of empathy. Summoning a level of discernment allows us to be judicious about what we say, catalyzing what will likely serve us, the listener, and our rapport.

The Problem Disownership Breakdown

Thanks to the work of the pioneers of the human potential movement such as Thomas Gordon, this protocol was born. These practitioners were very interested in understanding why relational breakdowns were prevalent even where there was ample trust in the relationship. The research revealed that 2 essential ingredients were missing to support resolution. The first missing piece was clarity about the nature of the problem. The second missing piece was the lack of clarity regarding who had the problem. Based upon the observations of couples experiencing a breakdown, a decision was made to define the problem as someone's unmet need. The person with the problem was then defined as the person with the unmet need. That person could be identified due to their feeling state. They likely were feeling angry, frustrated, disappointed, or hurt.

Two communication methods were introduced that would help facilitate both the expression of the unmet need and enhance the listener's ability to hear the unmet need. These skills include the use of "I-messages" and the elimination of "You-messages." I-messages are self-referential. They describe the speaker's experience and eliminate descriptions of the listener's character. The gift to listeners is that they remain in control of defining their own experiences during a breakdown. The second communication skill is reflective listening or simply acknowledging what is heard and eliminating interpretation and evaluation of what is said. An example is "I hear that you decided I didn't want to hear you when I left the room" rather than "I hear that you were mistaken when you insensitively decided I left the room to avoid hearing you."

We will be looking at 4 approaches to address relational breakdowns. To effectively employ these protocols, 4 distinct competencies will need to be developed. The first is being mindful of an attachment to be right or to win. The second is to be able to interrupt the attachment to be right or to win. The third is the use of "I-messages" and the elimination of "You-messages." The fourth is the use of reflective listening.

Since most of us are raised in families where problem disownership is practiced, employing the protocol with more self-referenced ways to talk can be challenging. To be clear about our needs can feel vulnerable since there's no guarantee that the listener will hear the need and want to be an ally regarding getting it met. When problem disownership is implemented, the person does not clearly identify their need. Instead, they employ blame, sarcasm, shame, and accusations directed at the other who allegedly played a role in not getting their need met.

Let's look at an example of problem disownership vs. problem ownership related to two people making an agreement that appears to be broken. **Person A** agrees to pick-up **Person B** at 6:30 PM for a 7:00 PM meeting. **Person A** arrives at 6:50. Leaving **Person B** feeling frustrated and angry.

Problem Disownership

> **Person B:** "You were supposed to pick me up at 6:30. I can't believe how irresponsible you are. I should have known better than to accept your offer of a ride."
>
> **Person A:** "You've been late picking me up in the past. I don't see what's your problem. Relax a little. You take this meeting too seriously."

Let's look more closely at this problem disownership exchange. First, **Person B** assumes an agreement was made with **A** for a 6:30 pick-up. **B** is not clear about his specific feelings and really not all that clear about the concrete consequences of his being late for the meeting. He moves to criticizing **A's** character, suggesting **A** is really the one with the problem. There's no real agreed-upon resolution. **A** defends his behavior by pointing out that **B** is one to talk considering his past actions. He then proceeds to evaluate **B's** unnecessary attachment to arriving on time for the meeting. If we expanded the exchange, it's likely that **B** would build a case in support for his need to arrive on time for the meeting. And of course, **A** could then assess that as somehow inappropriate. This kind of interchange goes on only too frequently with no one feeling heard, understood, and confident that a reliable resolution is in place.

Problem Ownership

> **Person B:** "My recollection is that we agreed you would pick me up at 6:30 PM for the meeting and it's now 6:50. I feel frustrated and angry. I will be missing the notes being read from the last meeting and reactions to those notes. If you have any awareness that you'll be late, please call me, so I can drive myself to the meeting."

> **Person A:** "I hear your frustration and anger about arriving late and missing the notes being read from the last meeting. I'm sorry that I caused that. The truth is that I spaced out and forgot I agreed to pick you up. I'm certainly willing to call you if I know I'm running late."

In this case, **B** begins by owning his recollection that an agreement was made rather than claiming it happened. This allows **A** to have a different memory. **B** is also very clear about his emotions and the concrete impact **A's** tardiness has upon him. He ends by making a clear and concrete request. It is always helpful when a resolution is framed in clear and concrete behavior. **A** acknowledges **B's** emotions and the problem **B** is articulating. He also takes responsibility for his role in the breakdown and agrees to the request to call **B** when he knows he will be late. An important key for **A** is the ability to hold his own personal worth although he broke an agreement with a friend leading the friend to have an unmet need.

Obviously, it helps a great deal if both the person with the problem (unmet need) and the listener are practicing problem ownership and the communication styles supporting the protocol. The good news is if 2 people have bought in on this method of addressing breakdowns, they should be able to successfully address over 90% of their upsets. All conversations won't necessarily go like the above example. However, as you commit to practicing, you will craft the process with your own language, and the more you make it your own, the more effective it will be.

The Conflict of Needs Breakdown

Let's look at a second recommendation for addressing breakdowns that came out of the human potential movement.

A conflict of needs does not occur as often as a breakdown with 1 person having an unmet need. A conflict of needs happens more frequently where there is frequent contact such as co-habiting and working together. Such a conflict occurs when each person can't imagine how they will get their need met if the other person gets their needs met. A key to this protocol working is to let go of being convinced that someone must lose and someone must win.

Let's look at the steps involved with this protocol:

Each person must be willing to interrupt their attachment to be right or to win. If your desire to be right is not apparent to you, then allow your attempts to influence inform you of your attachment to be right.

Each person defines his or her need in concrete behavioral terms. Example: Bob wants to see a film this Saturday at 8:00 PM with his spouse, Ellen. Ellen wants to attend the Ballet with Bob this Saturday evening at 8:00 PM.

Each person acknowledges the need of the other and the willingness to support that person getting their need met.

Together they generate possible solutions in support of both people getting their need met without evaluating a solution as unreasonable or inappropriate. Some possible solutions might include: Either Bob or Ellen choose a different evening to attend their event, each of them goes alone to their desired event, Bob goes with Ellen to her event and waits for the film to be aired on television, one of them goes to their event with a friend and the other goes alone, both attend their events with a friend, Ellen goes with Bob to the film waiting for the Ballet performance to happen in the neighboring city.

Prioritize two solutions that both Bob and Ellen can live with. A possibility might be that Ellen can accept going without Bob and attend with a friend and Bob is willing to see his film alone and a second option might be Ellen is willing to wait for the Ballet to be presented in the neighboring town and is willing to attend the film with Bob this Saturday. The key when prioritizing is that whatever is prioritized must be perfectly acceptable to both people. If there is difficulty finding even one solution, then returning to brainstorming is critical or involving a third person to help generate more options.

They choose one option that was prioritized and discuss how it will be implemented.

Meet after the option takes place to evaluate how successful the chosen alternative was.

The Conflict of Values Breakdown

A conflict of values can be a very challenging breakdown to address. Values represent what people cherish and what gives direction and purpose to their lives. Attempts to influence the other show up quite quickly when facing diverse values. It takes resiliency, acceptance, compassion, and curiosity to effectively work with a conflict of values. This is the kind of conflict that can cause a war.

Here are some steps to take when addressing a conflict of values, which are highlighted in Thomas Gordon's work:

Clarify and deepen your understanding of your own values. It's not advisable to step into the fray of an alleged values conflict without being very clear what your values are.

Clarify and deepen your understanding of the other's values. It's only too easy to have a strong emotional reaction to something that sounds contrary to what you believe. Reflect back to what you hear the other saying about what they value. Focus on distinguishing whether you are simply hearing a different value or a value contradictory to yours and in some way threatening to yours. A different value would be whether to raise children Catholic or Episcopalian. A contradictory value would be whether to raise children in the context of religious studies or no religion at all, which is much more difficult to manage.

Consider becoming a source of support for the other person's values. If you believe that the other person's values neither hurt them nor others, it may be beneficial to support their values. Much of the angst of a values conflict calms down when we feel supported in living our values.

Model the benefits of your values. Preaching or lecturing the benefits of your values will typically distance the listener and make them more resistant to either agree on the benefits or take them on and live with them. Modeling tends to have observers become more curious and interested in the values they are witnessing being lived. An example would be rather than preaching the value of regular physical exercise, just do it. An observer may notice your toned body, likely a more restful sleep, possibly fewer visits to the family doctor, more endurance during play and work, and living with less stress.

Become more accepting of the other person's values. This can be challenging if we have never considered the benefit of their values. The less the threat, the greater the likelihood of at least accepting the other's values. An example is my wife's value of walks and interaction with Nature. She sees Nature as her cathedral. It likely won't become my cathedral, yet I've noticed the relaxation and joy I experience walking our dog in the land preserve.

Learn from the other person's values. When the other person's values can be accepted, it can be easier to learn from the values. John reported being quite accepting of his wife's value regarding daily meditation. He started noticing that his wife's propensity to react was lessening. When he gave Barbara feedback concerning her appearing to be less reactionary, she explained that it might be due to her meditation. John began to explore meditation at his own pace and concluded that he was becoming less reactionary and decided to continue to meditate.

Attend to some trauma that might be influencing how the other's values are perceived. Theresa spoke of experiencing corporal punishment at school. She avoided any invitation her partner would offer regarding adult education or workshops.

She began psychotherapy sessions and discovered how much her school experience impacted how she viewed her partner's investment in learning and attending varied workshops. As she addressed her developmental trauma, she became less critical of her partner's investment in attending classes.

Build increased emotional resiliency. Often our values are held tightly in place by fear. We're convinced that something awful will happen if our values are not guiding what happens. It's always advisable to consider some early family messages we may have received that have us avoiding those who espouse a particular value. I recall my mother suggesting that folks who were financially well off were likely not good people, implying that they acquired money by means other than hard work. It took numerous encounters with wealthy folks who were trustworthy and kind to interrupt the old message. There are also questions that can support more understanding of a value that appears polarized to our own. Does it appear that this value will somehow hurt the person who purports it or harm others? What have I witnessed in the past when someone holds this value? Would I advocate this value to my children and grandchildren? Do I need to gather more information regarding this value to make an informed decision about it? Increased emotional resiliency shows up as a suppleness allowing us to hold values that on the surface may appear to be extremely different.

The Stories that Create Breakdown

These last 3 examples of relational breakdowns come directly out of the Human Potential Movement. "The Stories that Create Breakdown" is something I added. I began to notice how often I heard my clients reporting accounts of how much others rejected them, forgot them, dismissed them, excluded them, and criticized them. When I asked, "Did that person tell you they no longer wanted to relate to you?", the common response was, "Oh no, I just know that they don't want me in their life."

I would push the issue and suggest that they created a story about how that person feels about them and it doesn't mean that the person actually feels that way. The typical response was, "Oh yes, I do. I know they don't like me." I got more resistance when I suggested that they go to the individual and ask them to confirm or disconfirm the story they created. Person after person appeared to be more comfortable living with a story of rejection rather than taking the risk to discover the truth.

I began to see how often I lived in a story of rejection or exclusion without checking out my story with the person it's about. I decided that my resistance was about the fear of intimacy, it is quite intimate and vulnerable to go to someone we care for and disclose a hurtful story. The risk of course is that they might simply confirm that they need a break from our relationship. It quickly became obvious that my stories carried the power to separate me or have me avoiding the person. I was running the risk of creating separation from someone who had no investment in separation. I practice with my wife, friends, and colleagues. My hunch was correct. The practice of disclosing my stories deepened and supported intimacy. I feel some measure of fear, even now, after practicing over the past twenty years.

It may be wishful thinking, but I've noticed my clients become more willing to take the risk and tell someone the stories they created about them. The protocol is at least a bit easier to put together since it is commonly not about being right or winning. "I've created a story about us that I would like to share with you. I decided that you believe the content of the last book I wrote is not at all deserving of discussion." This is a recent story I brought to a friend. He quickly disconfirmed my narrative. I found his response to be trustworthy and was relieved that I was lifted from the burden of carrying a negative tale.

Maybe we should all practice going to people and telling them that we're carrying a story that they like us. It's time for some sweet stories to hit the airways. In the meantime, practice telling the not-so-sweet stories. It is such a burden to suffer unnecessary separation. Plus, I've noticed that if I'm not going to engage in power struggles and I don't trust my ability to address breakdowns, then various demonstrations of avoidance will guarantee the undermining of emotional intimacy. At best, something cordial and affable will ensue.

Some years ago, a friend defined me as very relational. I initially resisted such a description as it sounded very contrary to my extreme introversion. After giving it more consideration, I decided I was quite relational. It meant that I viewed meaningful relationships as a powerful container for self-discovery. Because of my investment, I was open to any tools that would help a relationship to remain a vital medium of personal growth.

I began using "I-messages" and reflective listening 45 years ago. I wanted to minimize power struggles and avoidance. I practice with my partner, my friends, colleagues, and students to whom I taught the skills. I was astonished to see my students co-creating and collaborating as they addressed philosophical issues. They saw one another as valuable learning resources.

I must admit, remaining mindful of my attachment to being right and winning remained considerably more elusive. At the time I was 29 and being well-mentored. With help, I became very curious about my far-reaching attachment to being right. I found a heroic, parentified child frightened to be uncertain. If I was wrong, how would I know how to live? If I wasn't right, who would want to be with me? If I wasn't right, who would hold the right answer? And maybe someone was depending upon me to be right? If I lost an argument, then what would it say about the beliefs guiding me to that point?

These many years later, I can still feel the presence of "You better be right!". On most occasions, I can quiet the quake in my stomach urgently entitling me to some alleged truth. However, I also have it be much less of a big deal when stumbling into uncertainty. It helps as I remember that I'm present with someone to learn and not to teach, which is not always comfortable for a Hero child.

I don't tarry much during a power struggle or take up residence in avoidance. It often means addressing a couple of breakdowns with someone each week. It can get intense, and I've been gifted by deep and meaningful relationships. I learn more about myself and the human condition. People tell me who they are more, and not just those on my therapeutic couch. Recently, our granddaughter told me about the challenges she faces as an introvert. It was a delight to be gifted with her transparency. I can witness the nuances of motivation whether advantageous or nefarious. Mostly, I'm glad to have the tools that allow me to more fully participate in relationships that matter to me, even if it means that they won't always work.

A Blessing for Rigorous Accountability

Working the messy material that comes in the way
of misunderstanding, hurt, disappointment, and the presence
of strongly diverse views will not resolve by attempts at
influence.
It's not true that most adults know how to address contentious
episodes in their relationships.
Let go of the illusion that a good relationship is inevitably
a bounty of harmony and good fortune.
A good relationship brings you closer to yourself.
It's a closeness that can only happen when you put down
your attachment to being right or to winning.
Now, you can come back to yourself in rigorous accountability.
With such responsibility,
the voice of blame becomes a distant echo.
Now, you know how to love by owning your own unmet needs,
and having yourself primarily responsible for meeting these needs.
Others are freed to take account of their own experience as you
suspend all allegations that they are somehow responsible for your
unlived life.

Chapter 15

Parenting

"Nothing has a stronger influence psychologically on their environment and especially on their children than the unlived life of the parent."

- Carl Jung -

One of the natural intentions we often carry from our families is to move from being a child to being a parent. We will explore the importance of moving from being a child to an adult while being a parent. Unfortunately, the contemporary version of parenting takes place in a nuclear family as opposed to an extended family. The hope is that friends, teachers, mentors, coaches, and neighbors fill in some of the inevitable blanks a nuclear family simply cannot address.

What is Parenting?

Several friends and colleagues responded to the question of parenting. "Parenting is the opportunity to serve something larger; and in the process of serving, I become larger. When I live parenting experiences consciously such as repeated frustration, powerlessness and my limitations, I become more of myself." Another mother offered, "Humbling, exhausting, heartbreaking and mind-numbing. More love than I ever imagined I could feel. It's a sacred contract between generations and the most important job of my life." A father looks at his parenting retrospectively, "Did I offer what was needed at appropriate times when they were ready or nearly ready to experience my offering? And was there a suitable foundational platform of attachment in place from which they could step?"

These responses to the question reveal the devotion, the love, the depth of the task, the mystery of the process, and how imperfect it will all unfold. We will reproduce how we were parented, compensate for how we were parented, and with a little luck, make an indispensable offering to our children. An old meaning of the word *parenting* is "to bring forth." I am quickly reminded of an old meaning of the verb *to educate* which is "to call forward." We can ask, what are we bringing forth or calling forward when we are parenting? And what is the most effective way to support this bringing and calling? I am reminded of the old Roman term *genius* which is not limited to intelligence. It reflects the spirit of a person, place, or thing. Of course, that leaves us with curiosity about what is the spirit of a child?

I have been gifted with 3 children as well as colleagues, friends, and clients who can easily be described as bearing large spirits. A child with a large spirit is curious and exhibits wonder and awe. They live close to their desire and a will that is eager to manifest. There is typically a measure of daring and boldness. They know how to live in a large love story. Large-spirited children know how to carry a sizable dream. Essentially, they are a lot, and they can be a lot to parent. However, regardless of the size of a child's spirit, the parental challenge remains the same - how to bring forth the spirit of the child while providing safety and freedom.

Attachment and Autonomy

Supporting a child's spirit coming forth calls for a balance of meeting needs for attachment and needs for autonomy. Parents cannot simply get this balance just right. We must remain corrective, reflecting the child's evolving needs and those of the other members of the family.

Attachment needs get met as a child turns to a parent and receives a level of emotional resonance. The child receives an energetic invitation to come closer to the parent. The closeness is composed of soft eye contact and a voice that modulates with the child's voice, often accompanied by acknowledgment, physical contact, and rhythmic breathing. Autonomy needs are met as the parent acknowledges the child's unique desires and wishes. Supporting autonomy does not mean all the child's wants are guaranteed. It does mean that the child is granted the entitlement to feel and voice a desire. The actual consummation of the desire will be determined by the available energy and time to support it, deciding how much parental support is required, and an evaluation of needs to support safety.

Again, the act of bringing the child's spirit forth greatly depends upon a commitment to support autonomy needs while reinforcing attachment needs. Carl, a 50-year-old father of 3, became seriously interested in bringing forth the spirit of his children.

"You know, one thing I worry about is how effectively my needs for attachment and autonomy were met as a child," Carl wondered, implying that his own childhood may have an impact on his parenting.

"Certainly, how we were parented can influence how we parent, and it's not necessary to perfectly reproduce it," I added, in the hope that Carl might feel free to tell his story and how it might relate to his parenting.

"Well, I'm thinking about an incident that happened when I was three of four years old. I went shopping with my mother and one of her friends. I remember that we were in Sears & Roebuck. My mother instructed me to stay close to her, and I wandered off to the sporting-goods department. When I returned to where I had left her, she and her friend were not to be found. I remember shaking and crying hysterically. My mother watched from behind a bin of sheets to teach me a lesson," Carl's voice trailed off, with the weight of his story sitting on my chest.

"Carl, I'm sorry that happened to you. Your mother was responsible to support your attachment needs as you explored your autonomy," I assured, realizing that Carl was sharing an integral piece of his attachment–autonomy story.

"I've noticed that I'm not always sure it's safe for me to venture out into the world. I know it's unreasonable, and I still carry the loss of attachment in Sears & Roebuck. Years later, my mother would show me pictures of her and me at some social event with me holding tight to her skirt. She would pronounce how successful her Sears & Roebuck caper was," Carl explained, his gaze dropping toward the floor, leaving energy of defeat in the air with his chest and shoulders caved in.

"Are you open to a recommendation?"

"Yeah, sure," he responded with more enthusiasm than I expected.

We proceeded to do guided imagery where he reproduced the incident. Only this time, his mother applauds his adventure to the sporting-goods department with welcoming open arms. I suggested he also reproduce the incident with the members in his therapy group. He returned to my office after the group therapy work, dripping in delight.

"Wow, it was one hell of an experience. I told the group what happened in Sears & Roebuck and what I needed that did not happen long ago. We were gathered in a large room. As I started to walk away from the group, I would turn back to look at them confirming they were still there. They would wave, telling me to have a good time and that they would be waiting for me and eager to hear about my adventure. I walked as far away from them as I could, turned around, and slowly made my way back. As I approached them, I heard cries of 'We missed you!', 'Did you have a good time?', 'It's so good to see you!', 'Come hang out with us!'", Carl proclaimed, sounding like a man who was returning from a long journey and being received with love and a deeply warm welcome.

"Carl, I've got to say, the work obviously served you," I offered, extremely pleased for the healing he welcomed into his life. Carl continued to father with a renewed faith that he could meet the attachment and autonomy needs of his children. He trusted that he would make certain corrections as needed and when losing his way, he knew he would ask for help.

Live Your Love

There are 2 wonderful ways to support your child's spirit to come forth. The first is to encourage what you see your child loving. It might mean letting go of directing your child toward what you love. It is a significantly loving act to not ask our children to somehow live our lives for us. For example, sometimes a child's love may be burdensome to the family and needs to be reconsidered. A child might love an activity like horseback riding which can be financially challenging and time-demanding. The key is not to allow the rest of the family to unduly suffer to support one person's love. Simply do your best to support some expression of what a child loves while not neglecting others.

The second way to support a child's genius to come forth is to live your love. First, if you're living your love, you won't need your child to do it for you. The modeling of living your love is a vivid demonstration of allowing your spirit to come forth. The child then has a wonderful map for allowing life to be guided by a heart's calling. Several years ago, when my son and I were sharing mutual acknowledgments on Father's Day, I recognized Jason's stewardship of his gifts and his dedication to living his love. He responded by saying, "With you as my father, do you think I had any other choice?" For me, it was a very endearing moment to remember, amidst the numerous misguided parental decisions I made.

Like all trustworthy recommendations, "Live Your Love" is not without a shadow. When a parent models living what is loved and does so with a significant degree of success either artistically, athletically, or professionally, a child giving witness to the loving and the success of the parent can easily feel intimidated and overwhelmed. This can lead to the child seeking some form of self-sabotage rather than feel the pressure to measure up to the parent's success story. The child can allow for academic failure, become alcohol or drug dependent and even mistakenly explore a gender transition to avoid the potential shame and disappointment of not measuring up. Parents living their love and succeeding in some only too obvious way need to pay particular attention to acknowledging and supporting the interests and love of the child, with strong encouragement to honor their own unique path.

3 Faces of Authority

Carrying parental authority can be a very confusing and challenging task. We can explore authority under 3 separate categories: **abuse**, **abdication**, and **causing growth**.

Abusing authority. Most of us are clear about what it means for authority to be abused. We have had enough experiences with authority figures shaming, ridiculing, bullying, and controlling the lives of others. Parental abuse is expressed by violating physical, emotional, and sexual boundaries. Parents abuse the power of their role when they are reproducing their childhood experience or feel inadequate or helpless.

Abdicating authority. Several years ago I was invited to Taos, New Mexico to address a group of men who were preparing to mentor boys. Our discussion quickly revealed a fervent commitment on behalf of the men to avoid abusing their authority at all costs. I suggested I was hearing an honorable attitude regarding a prohibition on abusing authority. I cautioned that the group may run a risk of compensating in the direction of abdication. The gathering quieted with a blanket of confusion regarding my caution. These well-intended men were risking moving head-on into abdicating their authority without appreciating the consequences. I went on to explain that abdicating authority means relinquishing it or giving it up.

There are typically 2 reasons that authority figures abdicate. The first is a strong desire not to abuse authority as characterized by these men. The second is to be liked or approved of by the recipients of our authority. I pointed out that abdicating authority has as many dire consequences as abusing it. Abdication creates confusion, anger, fear, and even a possible identity crisis for young people as they cannot find where they end, and the authority figure begins. It also suspends any modeling of how adults can cause growth by carrying authority. The fear and confusion result because children know they need to be guided and supported by adults holding authority or the power to create growth. Teenagers often address their fear of the loss of authority figures by joining gangs where the leaders pretend to know how to exercise authority. The anger children feel easily gets expressed in some form of acting out as they try to find the boundaries defining acceptable vs. unacceptable behavior. Instead of liking the adults who are abdicating, children are inclined to manipulate, sabotage, and resist any small measure of guidance offered. Abdicating adults soon resent the children in their care and feel overwhelmed and out of control. They even begin to do exactly what they were determined to avoid; they start abusing authority, attempting to liberate themselves from the perils of abdication.

Authority-causing growth. This third expression of authority goes unnamed and lacks clarity. As we saw earlier, an old definition of the word *authority* is "the one causing growth." Growth can refer to the individual being guided, as well as the growth of a family, group, or team. A second definition of the word is "a written or verbal statement that settles a question." We can consider *authority* to mean causing growth and taking a position that mitigates unnecessary confusion. Before exploring the first definition, let's look more closely at this idea of "a written or verbal statement that settles a question." Certainly, a parent has the responsibility to make a statement about any confusion pertaining to safety and unacceptable behavior. However, these statements need to be "I-messages" sent as the parent owning the problem as described earlier. The key again is that the problem is someone's unmet need, and typically it's a parent with the problem.

Authority-causing growth mostly happens through parental modeling and the kind of communication that happens between parent and child. There's modeling illustrating what it means to remain regressive and modeling that embraces growth. There's communication that tends to call forth a child's spirit and communication that inhibits it. In his book *P.E.T In Action*, Thomas Gordon outlines several significant communication roadblocks that inhibit growth in children: "Ordering, commanding, moralizing, preaching, advising, lecturing, judging, blaming, name-calling, analyzing, reassuring, probing and withdrawing." Just getting effective at eliminating these roadblocks is a life-long apprenticeship.

I recall a mentoring program I participated in during the 90s. As mentors, we worked hard at eliminating these roadblocks when communicating with the boys. None of us were quite sure what would take the place of the roadblocks. However, two options began to reveal themselves. The first was listening reflectively. In our own words, we would reflect what we heard. "Sounds like you're unhappy with what going on at home," or "I hear you saying that you feel uncomfortable speaking up in class." The second substitute was what I term "telling fool stories." Mentors would tell stories about mistakes, unfortunate decisions, and unfavorable liaisons. The boys listened attentively, curious about choices the men made, and lessons learned. My hunch is that the boys were rather captivated by the absence of preaching, lecturing, and advising.

Making it Happen

Besides eliminating roadblocks to growth-inducing communication, there are several essential components to authority-causing growth:

Teach children how to have a problem without acting out, either hurting themselves or someone else or damaging the environment. This lesson happens by modeling problem ownership by a clear description of the parent's unmet need, how it makes you feel emotionally, the concrete impact on your life, and a clear request. Gordon points out that clear "I-messages" describing problem ownership can be compromised or ineffective: "This happens if the parent doesn't describe the concrete effect the child's behavior has on the parent. Also, if the child doesn't feel heard when they have the problem, this might hinder how they respond when the parent has the problem.... It is inevitably tempting for parents to exercise the power of their role, which will not engender the child's trust. It also teaches children to resort to exercising power when they have it."

Employ concrete and logical consequences in response to unacceptable behavior. Concrete consequences are the impacts the physical world has upon a child's choices. Examples might include running on ice and getting bruised due to a fall, not wearing a coat and getting cold, getting too close to a fire and getting burnt, as well as not placing possessions in the storage area and not being able to find them. Concrete consequences can be a valuable resource for learning and becoming responsible. If parents allow children to learn from concrete consequences, then the parent will need to exercise enough discretion to determine if the concrete consequence in question is potentially too dangerous. The other consideration is how attached is the parent to how others will perceive him or her when they allow the child to learn from concrete consequences. I recall allowing my 8-year-old daughter to choose her attire for school. One day she stepped into the kitchen with stripes and polka dots clashing from top to bottom. Her mother and I looked at one another, decided there was no safety issue, and whether we could accept how the professional staff at school might see us. We wished her a good day at school; when she returned she asked her mother why her teacher wanted to know who chose her clothing. Logical consequences are the emotions and choices people make in response to behavior viewed as unacceptable. Logical consequences are also a valuable resource for learning. An example might be "I feel angry when I'm on the phone and you're yelling at me." Children want to learn what kinds of behavior elicit positive emotion and support for the building of rapport and what ones do not.

Listening Reflectively. When we listen reflectively, we don't add any new information to the message sent by the speaker. The result is that children feel heard and understood. They likely define the parent as a valued resource, and they learn what it means to feel genuinely understood. Effective listening is a valuable trust builder. They are also receiving good modeling for how to effectively listen.

Encourage. An old definition of the word en*courage* is "to inspire with courage." This form of inspiration at its best makes at least three offerings to children. The first is to view the challenges and defeats as statements about the nature of life and not testimonials of the child's deficiency. The second offering is to engender enough courage, to be honest about feeling scared, and to acknowledge if the child feels ready to act despite the fear or wait for another day. The key here is to frame being ready or not ready as honorable. The third offering of encouragement is holding the faith in who the child is and who they can become.

Modeling personal authority. The offering here is a map illustrating how children can support their growth. One significant demonstration of personal authority happens as parents refuse to rely on the power of their role to prove their maturity. Parents show that they know how to author themselves as they avoid power struggles with the child. This reveals a parent's nonattachment to winning or dominating as well as being manipulated. I highly recommend telling "fool stories." They are living testimony of your willingness to embrace your humanity and remain an apprentice to what life brings. Speak about your fear and how you support yourself. There is no better modeling than showing children how and to whom you turn for help.

A Blessing for Parenting

An empowered path for parents lies in the acceptance of
the one-way street of parenting.
Walking this road means we give, we encourage,
we model taking responsibility, and we hold our
children shamelessly accountable.
Our children are not responsible for making sure our
parenting is fulfilling and joyous.
Certainly, spending quality time with our children
is about acknowledging, listening,
and delivering messages of genuine care.
However, our gift to our children and to ourselves is a
well-lived life.
To witness such a thing offers children a map for honoring one's
longing, identifying and stewarding your gifts, allowing those gifts
to maximize a measure of service, and developing
relationships that truly matter to you.
Offer the children a large invitation to their humanity.
This happens as you tell Fool stories.
Narrate those times when you were only too ready to impress,
to demonstrate some prowess destined to make its mark
in the world,
and found yourself fumbling, falling quite short of
rousing applause and acclaim.
There is so much potential healing for our children
as they hear how much larger life is than their parents.

Chapter 16

Family Lessons about Endings and Death

"We are able to delude ourselves through our artful pretense. We all try to flee death. We attempt to run from our corruptible body and identify with the seemingly undying 'idea' or 'image' of our self. Although it is illusory, we are ingenious enough to manage for a time to have it be comforting. With this 'idea' of our self, we catapult ourselves out of the present. The fear of death generates an intense sensation of time as fleeting, as finite. We live on the run, greedily grabbing the next now, which we think preserves us. We live in fear of death, struggling to survive."

- *Kathleen Dowling Singh* -

Families are inevitably modeling and teaching how to handle things ending and dying. My family only made announcements pertaining to death – "Your Grandfather died." "There's a wake for your Uncle Joe." "Your Aunt Amelia's funeral is Saturday." I learned that death was a "no-talk" topic. There was no mention of how to handle loss or grief, what kind of support might be helpful, or it's simply okay to have questions about death and dying.

What I did learn was that my role of a Hero had me determined to conquer death. I wanted as much life as I could get my hands on. I have been trapped in the illusion that fighting death meant I was creating more opportunities to live. Isn't life about planning, intending, manifesting, generating, creating, and moving? As Singh points out in the above quote, "We catapult ourselves out of the present." The key is to minimize passivity, inertia, depression, loss and confusion, and inactivity - all indicators that death is close by. It took a while to figure out I neither knew how to live nor die.

It has taken me years for my eyes to see any skirmish with death also being combative with life. I stood proudly, convinced that I did all the living; and in the name of a fullness of life, I could keep death at bay. Little did I know that life was trying to live me. I could not feel the rhythm of life and death dancing together.

The Many Faces of Dying

There have been numerous places where I have engaged in warfare with death, of course never mindful of the casualties. Any expression of quiet, stillness and even serenity ran the risk of setting off sirens warning of the approaching enemy. Here are some of the more popular battlegrounds. Any form of illness would have me deploying a list of strategies aimed at denying any form of malady was taking place. My favorite militia included working more, eating more and at times doing my best at attempting to be sexual. All allegedly life affirming acts squelching any semblance of death from coming to roost.

Fatigue is another place where a skirmish could take place. The lethargy and passivity smelled of death. Again, time to summon the garrison of excessive activity in the name of work, play, travel, or socializing. Even a quiet moment might alert me to the presence of the grim reaper. There was certainly enough said in my family of origin regarding the nefarious nature of idleness. The suggestions all said something non-life-affirming was taking place, which easily could be a haven for the devil himself.

Let's look at some casualties accrued by doing battle with illness, fatigue, and quiet moments. These conditions are either making a request or providing something restorative that is either missing or compromised. When not responding to what these down times are offering, genuine self-care cannot be realized. Our immunity to fight disease is curbed when our capacity to care for ourselves is undermined. Our energetic capacity loses a robust edge. In short, our life force is diminished leaving us more prone to being depressed, unclear, lethargic, ill, apathetic, and remorseful.

When we don't prioritize rest, we are driven by urgency, excess, haste, and compensation. An overflowing amount of striving keeps us caught in laboring rather than allowing life to make its offering. Producing and giving are viewed as life-affirming while receiving is not.

I was duly enthralled with my approved life, incessantly doing. It's taken decades for me to acknowledge I really don't know life at all. I failed to see how much there was to receive. Receiving felt a little too close to death. I didn't understand what someone receiving was really doing. On the other hand, giving is so active and life-promoting. Receiving simply became another casualty.

I decided to watch people who were receiving. I started to sense a measure of humility, acceptance, and gratitude expressed by receivers. Their acceptance showed itself in their lack of protest, resistance, and digression. I also noticed a softness in their cheeks and something unassuming in their persona which if it had a voice might sound like, "Life likes me and wants to treat me kindly." Their humility showed itself as an acceptance of what was taking place. Their task appeared to be to allow the giving to happen.

I began to realize that when I was doing the giving, the receiver was allowing me to be my giving-self. I started to feel grateful for either being a giver or receiver. In either role, I was receiving from the other the chance to be myself.

The Dance

The first hint that life and death were in a dance happened in my early 40's while studying Kung Fu. We students were practicing punching. Just as I was convinced that my punches were transcending the sensei's expectations, I heard, "What are you doing?"

"Practicing punching," I responded, well aware that I had failed to exceed his expectations.

The sensei went on to point out that my punches were losing a great deal of power. He instructed me to completely open my hand while holding it in the chamber, alongside my right hip. He explained that the power of the punch resulted as I gradually made a fist while thrusting my hand toward the target. There was a powerful metaphor staring me in the face. Power happens because of a movement from still and soft to hard and accelerating and back again.

It has taken years for me to begin to let go of the schism between active and passive. I begin to see the dance of life, the flow of movements between soft and still to hard and advancing and back again. The rhythm is timed by my hunger, fatigue, age, desire, and of course, what life is asking of me. Our cadence is certainly not perfect, and I'm not afraid anymore of napping. I let go into the faith that my rest will yield more of me and more life.

It may be that the faces of death simply ask for a tempo, allowing what I intend to dance with what life brings to me. Sometimes what life brings is larger than what I would have made happen. When that occurs, I can either protest life's offering or allow life to live me. Everything from what another person issues in my direction to what Nature presents and even my next breath are examples of life living me. I'm letting life live me as I sit here on the beach. Life provides a showcase of waves pounding the beach, the softness of the sand, a variety of birds soaring and diving, the warmth of the sun on my skin, and a cool ocean breeze seemingly dedicated to mitigating too much heat.

How easy it would be to declare that I'm responsible for this day at the shore, all the time forgetting it is my passivity that allows for the breadth of the experience. Beauty is one of the most unfortunate casualties when warring with death. When I can suspend intention and some ensuing action, pausing allows me to receive some expression of beauty trying to reach me.

Holding On & Letting Go

The dance of life and death gets lost as we decide that they are an unmanageable polarity having little or nothing to do with one another. We can consider holding on as reflective of life and letting go as an expression of death. When we hold on, we are guided by a desire, an intention, and some ensuing action. When let go, we suspend our attachment to an intention and relinquish some desired outcome. We allow life to live us.

For years, I held myself in a snare disallowing for making peace with letting go. The older I became, the more effective I was at identifying internal and external resources in support of what I desired to manifest. I didn't realize that this increased acumen regarding generating resources would keep me more deluded about holding on and letting go. I was convinced I could now control more than ever. I refused to find the exit door out of my distortion. Rather than issue an armistice with letting go, I took up sanctuary as I lamented how cruel life could be with me. I allowed regret to shield me from whatever was occurring other than my wishes. It soon became apparent that the woeful path was paved with feeling like a victim.

I believe that learning how to hold on and let go is a life-long spiritual practice. We were recently visited by a friend, his wife, and three children. He and I are currently engaged in a unique professional opportunity, one that leads to robust conversations. It became immediately obvious that if he and I indulged in shop talk, it would alienate his family and my wife, so we both let go. Over a 4-hour period, he and I shared one or two brief professional stories.

I sensed the spirit of woefulness preparing to descend upon me. However, I was able to sustain a measure of curiosity regarding what was present in lieu of my desire. I witnessed how engaged he was with his children, causing me to pause, beginning to wonder about losses pertaining to my children. I appreciated hearing his spouse's willingness to step into the unknown concerning her professional life and the gentle invitations my wife offered her to share her thoughts and feelings.

Life continues to remind me that there might be hope for me. I'm more okay taking on this apprenticeship to holding on and letting go. I have no idea what mastery might look like and I'm content to be a devoted apprenticeship. Who knows, in whatever time I have left on the planet I might learn a bit about living and dying.

The Dignity and Messiness of Dying

"I don't want to die like an asshole!" an old friend cried out to his spouse several weeks before he took his last breath. My friend was bright, extremely creative, and loving, with his last days offering testimony to rejecting an inauspicious death - one without dignity. What does a death lacking dignity look like? Is it protesting the inevitable, even to our last breath?

As Dylan Thomas encourages:

"Do not go gentle into that good night,
Old age should burn and rave at the close of day;
Rage, rage against the dying of the light."

Or could a dignified death be a bit more tranquil and possibly more welcoming as suggested by Emily Dickenson?

"Because I could not stop for Death-
He kindly stopped for me –
The Carriage held but just Ourselves –
And Immortality."

Even those believing in reincarnation likely don't remember how they died in past lives. So how do we prepare for something we do only once in this life? Is there any way to acquire some practice dying?

Practice Dying and Birthing

Living in a death-denying culture places an immense burden upon our relationship to dying. To deny death is to suggest on some level it's simply not real. Our efforts to bring meaning to dying need to be counter-cultural whereby we personalize and reclaim the dying experience. We live with a myriad of euphemisms for the word *die*. A marriage *ends,* work is *terminated,* a project *closes*, a school year is *complete,* the weekend *finishes* and time to register *expires*. Although there is nothing inappropriate about our euphemisms, when pushed they can mask the loss and grief associated with so many different endings.

Maybe It's not very easy to get honest about life being a series of moments coming (*birthing*) and going (*dying*), or about life offering opportunities to practice closure. Handling *small deaths* (closures) can be messy. We will likely have feelings of not getting it right, not doing enough, or doing too little. We'll feel rejected, forgotten, guilty for leaving or perhaps holding too many regrets to count. And what about being overwhelmed by the uncertainty of the moment? Often a job changes without our really acknowledging the transition. Neighbors die without recognition of those left behind. People move away and nothing is said about the loss.

We often leave relationships abruptly without being clear about our choice. This sudden and undisclosed departure in social media is called "ghosting." Isabella Chan's recent *Hartford Courant* article sites the research conducted by Professor Royette Dubar and Jhanelle Oneika Thomas focusing on this closure avoidant phenomenon so common today. It occurs when a person decides without explanation to cut off all online and/or in-person communications. "When individuals engage in ghosting, they're almost robbing themselves, and the ghostee, of opportunities to grow, to mature and to have the hard, maybe messy, very important interpersonal labor that will ultimately reveal healthy communication and healthy relationships," says Dr. Dubar.

She concludes that attending to these small deaths allows us to have richer lives. What's more, it's just good death practice! Let's challenge ourselves to possess enough emotional resiliency to feel and metabolize the messy feelings generated by dying and to hold enough receptivity and faith to open to the ensuing birth.

Maybe, we've been haunted by these ghosting experiences since Paul Simon bellowed out the tune "Fifty Ways to Leave Your Lover" in 1975, none of which suggested something clear and honest. The haunting refrain includes *Slip out the back Jack, make a new plan Stan, you don't need to be coy, Roy, just set yourself free, hop on the bus Gus, you don't need to discuss much, just drop off the key Lee and set yourself free.* Apparently, a successful exorcism of Simon's ghosting experiences has not happened over the past 46 years.

Softening into the Table of Life and Death

As I climbed onto my physical therapist's table, I heard him say, "See if you can soften into the table." Soften into the table? Am I being hard on his table? I simply never heard anyone suggest I should soften onto a table. In any case, feeling somewhat embarrassed about not knowing what the hell he was asking of me, I was determined to exhibit my prowess as a patient.

Not having any clue about what I was to do which might resemble softening into the table, I looked at my hands out in front of me, palm down, and decided to spread my fingers. My hands seemed to follow suit as they began to easily unfold. My forearms and shoulders appeared to easily join in on this softening process. As they did, so did my chest, stomach, and legs. I hoped I was softening and softening well, when I heard the therapist say, "Good job."

The statement, "See if you can soften into the table," stayed with me, as if asking something from me. It wouldn't go away. After several weeks of feeling haunted by the phrase, I began to wonder if I was being asked to make a metaphorical leap from the therapist's table. Suddenly, without intention, the thought, "What about softening into the table of life," filled me with moving inspiration.

I began to wonder what might happen if we soften into the table of life and death as well. Softening into the therapist's table made my body more receptive to therapeutic touch. Maybe softening into the table of life might have me more open to how life can touch me. I began to reflect how many times my tightening, my hardening, and torque of my intensity insulated me from human warmth, love, affection, kindness, appreciation as well as being touched by music and beauty.

Could it be that softening into the table of life meant more life? What about being in the presence of an act of cruelty or danger? Well, I can always harden up with some boundary, securing safety. I again recalled my old sensei explaining that that the power of a punch happened because the fist went from soft to hard, not hard to hard. Soft to hard, not hard to hard.

Learning to Die

I began to wonder how softening into the table of life might teach me how to die. I decided that dying is mostly about letting go and that there would be plenty of opportunities to practice letting go of austerity and intensity.

It has taken me quite a few years to accept how much of my lived experience is out of my control. It has been a sizable concession to admit how little power my intentions have produced. I see now that life is mostly a series of opportunities to respond to people, situations, and events. I have made a measure of peace with the notion that I am he who can respond with my values, my desire, and beliefs. Responding often calls for letting go of my preferred intentions and remain curious about what a situation may be asking of me. Of course, I'm typically a bit surprised, when it is clearly asking little or nothing from me. However, it's simply another chance to let go and practice dying.

I recall my initial reaction to the idea that letting go is about learning to die. How can letting go of a concrete life situation be like actually dying? Don't we know the likely outcome of letting go of concrete events while what happens after our bodies cease to function seems to remain a mystery?

It took a while for me to vigilantly track my ego's investment in the illusion that I know what will occur when I let go of some tangible happening. Of course, there is a level of probability if I drive in the US on the right side of the road, I'll make it to my destination. The nuance in such a belief is that I slide my arrival into a guarantee rather than holding a level of probability and therefore doubt. It may be worth considering how mysterious both living and dying might be.

It simply may be worth entertaining the limits of our intentions. It doesn't mean we should not intend with aspirations of being creative and in service. However, it does mean getting honest about how little is actually in our control, learning to control what we can and letting go of the rest. The 13th century Sufi Rumi suggested, "Life is a balance of holding on and letting go."

Recently, while reading a book about aging by Parker Palmer, a statement in the text caught my attention and began haunting me days after the initial reading. Palmer said that as he looked back upon his life, he could rightfully say, "I've been a very lucky guy." I've heard that phrase endless times along the way, possibly reflecting a man's fortuitous evening at the Casino.

I have also heard the statement as a reflection of false modesty, as a man performs beyond all expectations and refuses to take some measure of credit. The refusal often lands on me as a manipulation aimed gathering more adulation from the crowd. However, I never heard it as way of describing a life well lived. Why was I now willing to ascribe deeper meaning to a statement that always sounded like a cheap cliché?

Parker Palmer has written numerous books and has received many honors and awards. He's also responsible for the creation of the Center for Courage and Renewal, which is a retreat center in South Carolina. As I made my way through his latest book, *On the Brink of Everything: Grace, Gravity and Getting Old*, I found the author to be both honest and humble. But what about, "I've been a very lucky guy"? The statement now held a message of sincere gratitude. It also spoke of Palmer's humility as he resists ascribing credit only to himself for his accomplishments, as well as implying he was open to receiving support and help. There is also an implicit acceptance of the immensity of life and the need to be helped along the way. I find it extremely helpful to my aging to have a man speaking in a way that implies life owes him nothing. It suggests he was willing to serve life as opposed to being self-serving.

I seem to be hearing and seeing very simple things that offer so much to me, like "I've been a very lucky guy." I see how one single breath can teach so much about life and death. I inhale taking life in, and I exhale letting go of life, only to be offered another breath of life. I'm practicing now what I call a short prayer, "I am a very lucky guy, learning to soften into all that life has given me." I seem to believe it in very small incremental pieces. And I am very comfortable having it be my psycho-spiritual task.

References and Permissions

Chapter One

Virginia Satir - https://www.facebook.com/family.matters.parenting. 2019. "Best Family Quotes by the Amazing Virginia Satir | Family Matters." Ronitbaras.com. January 30, 2019. https://www.ronitbaras.com/family-matters/parenting-family/best-family-quotes-by-virginia-satir/.

Chapter Two

Excerpt(s) from CHILDREN OF SANCHEZ by Oscar Lewis, copyright © 1961 by Oscar Lewis, renewed 1989 by Ruth Lewis. Used by permission of Random House, an imprint and division of Penguin Random House LLC. All rights reserved.

Chapter Three

Excerpt(s) from JUST LISTEN by Sarah Dessen, copyright © 2006 by Sarah Dessen. Used by permission of Viking Children's Books, an imprint of Penguin Young Readers Group, a division of Penguin Random House LLC. All rights reserved.

Chapter Four

Elizabeth Kubler-Ross- n.d. EKR Foundation. Accessed June 5, 2021. https://www.ekrfoundation.org/elisabeth-kubler-ross/quotes/.

Chapter Five

Excerpt(s) from DARING GREATLY: HOW THE COURAGE TO BE VULNERABLE TRANSFORMS THE WAY WE LIVE, LOVE, PARENT, AND LEAD by Brené Brown, copyright © 2012 by Brené

Brown. Used by permission of Gotham Books, an imprint of Penguin Publishing Group, a division of Penguin Random House LLC. All rights reserved.

Bradshaw, John. 2005. *Healing the Shame That Binds You*. Health Communications.

Gershen Kaufman - *SHAME: The Power of Caring,* pg. 12, Author Gershen Kaufman, Published by Schenkman Books, Inc. ISBN: 0870470078

Chapter Six

F. Scott Fitzgerald - "Show Me a Hero and I'll Write You a Tragedy." 2015. The Odyssey Online. June 22, 2015. https://www.theodyssey online.com/show-me-hero-i-ll-write-tragedy.

Chapter Seven

Fletcher, Giovanna. *Billy and Me*. Macmillan, 5 APR. 2016.

Sharon Wegscheider Cruse - Wegscheider-Cruse, Sharon. 1981. *Another Chance*. Palo Alto, CA: Science and Behavior Books, INC.

Chapter Eight

Glynis Sherwood - Sherwood, Glynis. 2019. "12 Steps for Family Scapegoat Healing." Glynis Sherwood. Glynis Sherwood. May 17, 2019. https://glynissherwood.com/12-steps-for-family-scapegoat-healing/.

Chapter Nine

S. Rufus - "Arrested Development." n.d. Psychology Today. Accessed September 12, 2021. https://www.psychologytoday.com/us/blog/stuck/200812/arrested-development.

Sharon Wegscheider-Cruse Wegscheider-Cruse, Sharon. 1981. *Another Chance*. Palo Alto, CA: Science and Behavior Books, INC.

Chapter Ten

Jessica Evans - "Parentification – Forced to Grow up Too Soon." 2018. I Am 1 in 4. April 28, 2018. https://iam1in4.com/2018/04/emotionally-damaging-parentification/.

Chapter Eleven

Excerpt(s) from WOMEN AND THEIR FATHERS by Victoria Secunda, copyright © 1992 by Victoria Secunda. Used by permission of Dell Publishing, an imprint of Random House, a division of Penguin Random House LLC. All rights reserved.

Chapter Twelve

James Hollis - Hollis, James. Letter to Paul Dunion. 2023. "A Quote." Email, July 14, 2023.

Thomas Moore - From *Care of the Soul* by Thomas Moore. Copyright (c) 1992 by Thomas Moore. Used by permission of HarperCollins Publishers.

Paul Tillich and F Forrester Church. 1999. *The Essential Tillich: An Anthology of the Writings of Paul Tillich*. Chicago, Il: University of Chicago Press.

Chapter Thirteen

Used with permission of Hazelden Publishing, from The Gifts of Imperfection, Brene Brown, 2020; permission conveyed through Copyright Clearance Center, Inc.

Chapter Fourteen

Aristotle - "Anyone Can Become Angry, That's Easy - Physician's Weekly." n.d. Www.physiciansweekly.com. Accessed July 14, 2021. https://www.physiciansweekly.com/anyone-can-become-angry/.

Chapter Fifteen

Carl Jung - Christian, James. 2009. "The Impact of the Unlived Life of the Parent | True Fatherhood." True Fatherhood. July 19, 2009. http://www.truefatherhood.org/articles/the-impact-of-the-unlived-life-of-the-parent/.

Gordon, Thomas, and Judith Gordon Sands. 1976. *P.E.T. In Action.* New York: Wyden Books.

Chapter Sixteen

From Grace in Dying by Kathleen D. Singh. Copyright(c)1998 by Kathleen Dowling Singh. Used by permission of HarperCollins Publishers.

Dylan Thomas - Thomas, Dylan. 1947. "Do Not Go Gentle into That Good Night." Poets.org. 1947. https://poets.org/poem/do-not-go-gentle-good-night.

Emily Dickenson - Academy of American Poets. 2019. "Because I Could Not Stop for Death (479) by Emily Dickinson - Poems | Poets.org." Poets.org. 2019. https://poets.org/poem/because-i-could-not-stop-death-479.

Hartford Courant - "Ghosting – the Silent, Unexplained Method to Ending Relationships – Has Negative Impact on Both Parties and Can Stunt Emotional Growth, Wesleyan Study Finds." 2021. Hartford Courant. December 20, 2021. https://www.courant.com/2021/12/20/ghosting-the-silent-unexplained-method-to-ending-relationships-has-negative-impact-on-both-parties-and-can-stunt-emotional-growth-wesleyan-study-finds/.

Simon, Paul. *50 Ways to Leave Your Lover.* Columbia Records, 1975.

Rumi - Mani, Mukesh. 2017. "Life Is a Balance between Holding on and Letting Go – Rumi." OutofStress.com. December 18, 2017. https://www.outofstress.com/life-is-a-balance-rumi/.

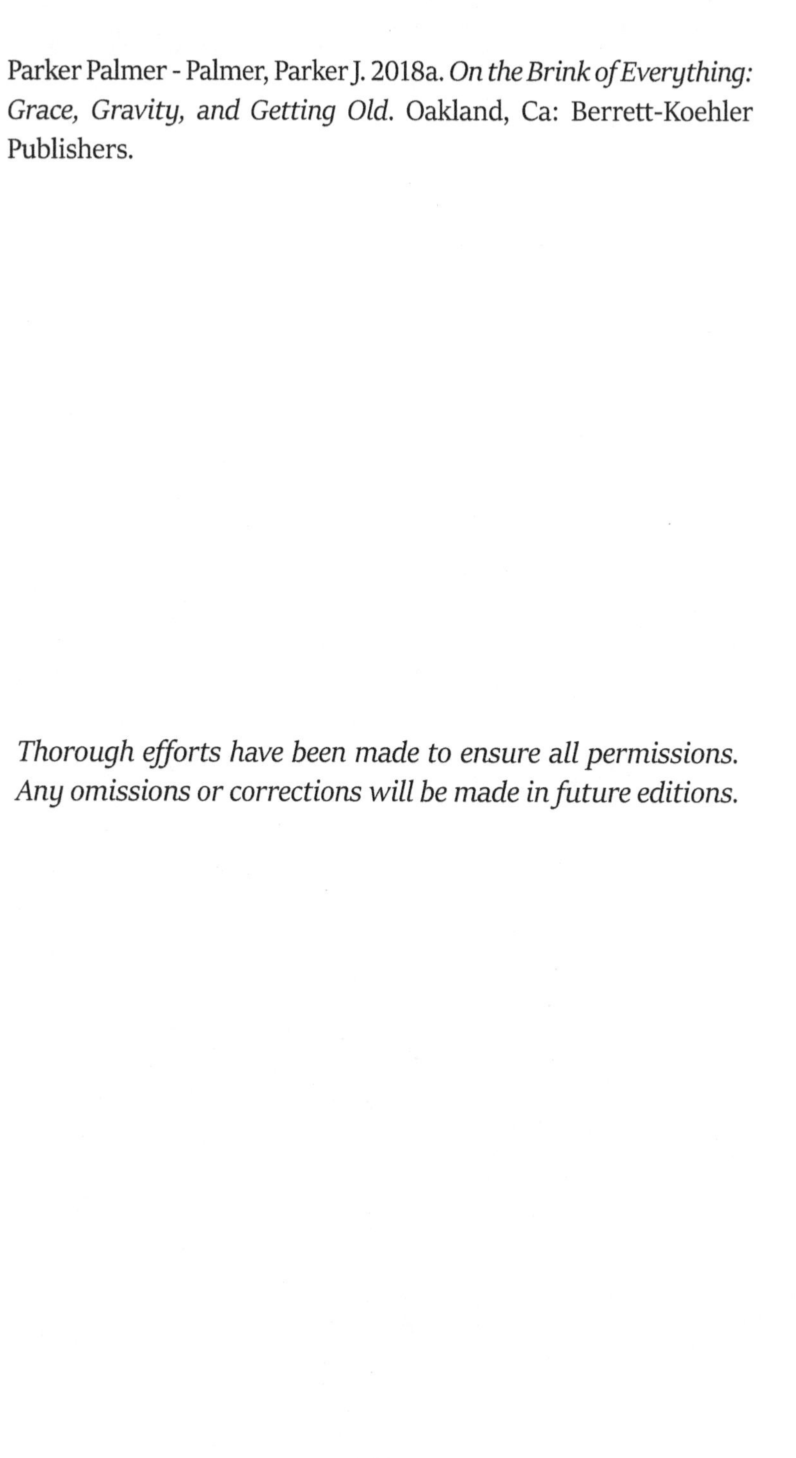

Parker Palmer - Palmer, Parker J. 2018a. *On the Brink of Everything: Grace, Gravity, and Getting Old.* Oakland, Ca: Berrett-Koehler Publishers.

Acknowledgments

I typically do not write about topics in which I feel well versed. My writing reflects the inquiries in which I live.

I want to acknowledge and express deep appreciation for the friends and colleagues who accompany me in these inquiries. The list includes Thom Allena, Gary Blaser, Hilorie Baer, Ray Di Capua, Peter Drake, Amy Elizabeth Fox, Margaret Harris, James Hollis, Alex Kuilman, Michael Lierow, Ester Martinez, Deirdre O'Connor, Michael Paprocki, Norcott Pemberton, Sven Peterson, Wendy Shami, Jennifer Jondreau-Thompson, and Andrea Borman Winter.

I have been immensely gifted and privileged to serve students who have inspired my curiosity and wonder. A special thanks to Connie Jones Dunion who joins me in our shared inquiries reminding me to carry my sense of intrigue with a light heart.

These folks offer me a cherished opportunity to pause and recalibrate in the direction of what truly matters. My need to demonstrate and prove something is mitigated by their devotion to interrupt an attachment to artificiality. Inevitably, such a devotion means welcoming a measure of vulnerability which lives at the core of any worthwhile inquiry. I am especially thankful for their humility which affords them the opportunity to release an attachment to a possible bypass.

Acknowledgments

About Atmosphere Press

Founded in 2015, Atmosphere Press was built on the principles of Honesty, Transparency, Professionalism, Kindness, and Making Your Book Awesome. As an ethical and author-friendly hybrid press, we stay true to that founding mission today.

If you're a reader, enter our giveaway for a free book here:

SCAN TO ENTER
BOOK GIVEAWAY

If you're a writer, submit your manuscript for consideration here:

SCAN TO SUBMIT
MANUSCRIPT

And always feel free to visit Atmosphere Press and our authors online at atmospherepress.com. See you there soon!

About the Author

Paul Dunion, EdD, is a teacher, author, and psychological healer committed to remaining mindful of life as a mysterious and unpredictable journey. A steadfast believer in the power of community, Paul founded Boys to Men, a mentoring program for teenage boys, and COMEGA, the semi-annual Connecticut Men's Gathering now in its 30th year of service. Paul currently is a Senior Consultant and Transformative Faculty with Mobius Executive Leadership. Paul has spent over forty years offering therapeutic support to folks committed to interrupting the darker elements of family legacies as well as holding on to the best of those legacies. Storytelling, facilitating and writing are some of Paul's strongest gifts. He regularly contributes to various online platforms. *Family: In Search of Genuine Belonging* is his eighth book. Paul lives in eastern Connecticut with his wife, Connie, and dog, Kody.

About the Author

www.ingramcontent.com/pod-product-compliance
Lightning Source LLC
LaVergne TN
LVHW091306150826
845673LV00006B/1555

9798891321113